Life as a Pioneer

by Bob Rybak

illustrated by Susan Kropa

FS-10140 Life as a Pioneer
All rights reserved–Printed in the U.S.A.
Copyright © 1994 Frank Schaffer Publications, Inc.
23740 Hawthorne Blvd.
Torrance, CA 90505

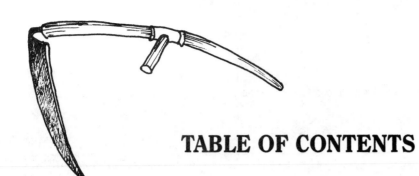

TABLE OF CONTENTS

INTRODUCTION

The American pioneer has had a tremendous impact on Americans today. Such a statement seems obvious enough when we consider that it was the American pioneer who opened and tamed frontier areas that are sprawling metropolises today. Looking beyond the obvious, however, we see that the characteristics of the American pioneer are the same characteristics that are valued today.

Have your students think of any modern American who is considered successful today whether that success is financial or professional. Have them list the characteristics of that person, and chances are the list will contain the same characteristics we associate with the American pioneer. These traits would include self-sufficiency, fierce independence, diligence, innovative thinking, persistence, courage, and willingness to take risks. Whether in business, industry, science, education, sport, or entertainment, the people we admire most will display one or more of those characteristics. Who we are as Americans today is firmly rooted in who we were during the frontier days of American history. Simply put, we identify with that pioneer and to this day we continue to emulate the characteristics that made the pioneer successful.

Studying the pioneer era of our American history needs to move beyond identification of special events. To link our past with our present, students need to understand who the pioneer was and what his/her life was like. Students need to make cognitive connections between their lives and the life of a pioneer if they are to develop deep understanding of what America is and who Americans are.

How to Use This Book

Life as A Pioneer is divided into 10 chapters; each one being one aspect of pioneer living. Taken as a whole they help to create a picture of the pioneer experience. Each of the 10 chapters is divided into smaller units. For example, the chapter on the pioneer is divided into units on 1) describing the American pioneer, 2) the first-wave pioneer, 3) the second-wave pioneer, and 4) the third-wave pioneers. Each unit has information specifically selected to be passed on to students along with activities that allow them to interact with the information.

There is no special formula to follow when integrating the information with the activities. You can provide the activity as a lead-in to a concept or first provide the information and follow it up with an activity. Feel free to change the activities to fit your class circumstances.

Following the 10 chapters is a set of resource materials and an index to the activities. The resource material includes a list of books, both fiction and nonfiction, that students can use to supplement their study of the pioneer era. Also included is a list of computer programs on the pioneer era. The index provides a quick reference to all activities. It also provides a list of subjects and skills to which each activity relates. In developing your plans, therefore, you will be able to more easily integrate the study of the colonial period with other subjects.

Fitting the Curriculum

Accountability, one of the more dominating movements today in education, has the undesirable side effect of constricting the experiences we provide students in the classroom. This happens because we as teachers are compelled to design our teaching to facilitate clear evaluation of all material covered. As a consequence, activities that do not conform to easily graded paper-and-pencil evaluation methods often are seen as enrichment (a.k.a. extra stuff we don't have time for).

Teaching students the total pioneer experience is not a frill. It is not enrichment. It is as important as all the dates and events they commit to memory. Even more so. The one barrier most teachers see to including this material in a unit on the pioneer time period is that it does not lend itself to traditional evaluation methods. This might be true, but it does not prevent a teacher from incorporating it into the unit.

Evaluating what students learned from the activities can be done in valid and traditional ways. The most common is to have them write a reaction paper to an activity. If students are unfamiliar with this form of evaluation then they need some guidelines. For example, they will need to know the objective of the writing. They will need to understand that they must reflect on what they learned from the activity and be able to explain how it relates to the pioneer experience and their own lives.

Many of the activities are designed to have students interact with one another and then report back to the class. Both phases can become part of the evaluation process. Teachers can observe the discussion and note contributions as well as listen to and grade the final presentation.

Additional activities are available in this book's companion entitled *Life as a Colonist*. By looking over the information and activities in that book you will easily find more material which easily relates to your class' study of life as a pioneer.

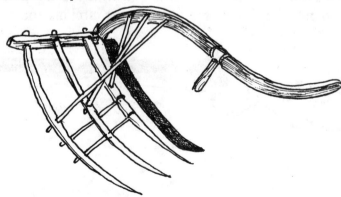

CHAPTER ONE
The Frontier

Where Was the Frontier?

The American frontier was an area of the United States that both grew and shrank in size throughout the sixteenth, seventeenth, eighteenth, and nineteenth centuries. It grew as acquisitions were made and explorers ventured into previously unmapped areas extending the frontier boundaries. It shrank as pioneers settled the land and created farms, towns, and cities. The first step in helping students understand the life of a pioneer is getting them to realize that the American frontier was several different places at different times in American history. Each location and time had distinctive elements of life style

The first settlers who came to America were the colonists. They settled along the Atlantic seaboard and did their best to recreate the English way of life in America. Settlements in this frontier began at the coast and extended to the fall line of the Appalachian Mountains. The fall line is an imaginary line that connects waterfalls and rapids of the mountain range. It prevented further navigation on the rivers and thus further settlement. The contact that these people had with England, however, prevented a true frontier life style from developing. Instead, a unique colonial life style was created that is more thoroughly explored in this book's predecessor entitled *Life as a Colonist*. The seaboard colonies became sufficiently well-established by 1700 to bring that frontier to an end.

The first American frontier was an area that today we would call the Piedmont. It has also been called the "Old West." The Piedmont was about 1300 miles long, extending from New York to Georgia, and included many interior valleys. It extended from the fall line to the crest of the Appalachian Mountains. Consequently, the Appalachians were one of three barriers that prevented pioneers from settling farther west. A second barrier to expansion was French possession of that land, and the third was the presence of native Americans who forcefully resisted encroachment. The Piedmont frontier opened around 1700 and by 1776 had become sufficiently settled to no longer be called a frontier.

The second frontier was the Eastern Mississippi region. Following the French and Indian War, the land from the Appalachian Mountains to the Mississippi River became available, and the American frontier grew to include all land from the Appalachian crest to the Mississippi. The British, who acquired the land as a result of the war, drew up the Proclamation of 1763. This proclamation reserved land west of the Appalachian Mountains for all native Americans. The pressure to settle this land as well as the breaking of ties with England during the American Revolution created a change in policy. The settling of Kentucky, Tennessee, Ohio, and Louisiana developed quickly during and just after the American Revolution. The War of 1812 brought an end to active resistance by native Americans who had suffered many defeats by aligning themselves with the British. After the war, Indiana, Illinois, Michigan, and Wisconsin in the North as well as Alabama, Mississippi, and Florida in the South were settled. By 1840 this frontier area was so well developed that it ceased to be considered a frontier.

During the settling of the Eastern Mississippi Frontier, a land purchase dramatically changed the size of the American frontier. That purchase was the acquisition of the Louisiana Territory from France. Almost overnight, the size of the United States doubled, and a new frontier was created that was larger than any other obtained by the United States. Settlement of it would require government incentives, political action, improved transportation, improved farming and mining technology, and elimination of land claims by native Americans. The Louisiana Territory contained such a variety of environments that settlement by pioneers encompassed many very different life styles.

The third frontier area to be settled included part of this Louisiana Purchase. Known as the Western Mississippi Frontier, it extended from the Mississippi River to approximately the ninety-eighth meridian. It is at this longitude that a much drier climate prevented successful settlement because of poor farming conditions. Actual settlement of these lands began in the early nineteenth century but took off in the 1830s. Political blockades, such as questions of statehood (free or slaves) and rights of ownership (Mexico vs. Texas), slowed settlement more than any natural barriers. As with other frontiers, though, native American resistance was a factor in the settlement of these lands. In Iowa and Minnesota eventual treaties, stemming from conflicts with Sauk, Fox, and Sioux, provided for quick settlement. By 1860 Minnesota, Iowa, Missouri, and Arkansas all had attained statehood, thus ending their frontier days. Parts of Texas, Kansas, and Nebraska had also undergone enough settlement in their eastern half to end their days of being called *frontier*.

It would appear that the development and settling of the American frontier followed a single time line and was consistently westward in expansion. This was not so. The fourth frontier area was the Pacific frontier. It was explored and developed simultaneously with the previous two frontiers. The Pacific frontier included land from the Pacific Ocean to the two mountain ranges that make up the Pacific Coast ranges—the Cascades and the Sierra Nevada. It was made up of California and the Oregon Territory. As early as 1542, Spain was exploring the California coast. In the 1760s and 1770s Spaniards set up a chain of missions throughout northern California. In 1821 Mexican independence resulted in California becoming property of Mexico, but following the Mexican War, California was ceded to the United States. The discovery of gold in 1848 brought such a huge influx of miners and settlers that by 1850 little of California could be called frontier. In fact, California became a state in 1850.

The land known as Oregon began as a huge portion of land extending from California north to what is today British Columbia. Russia, England, Spain, and the United States all laid claim to some portion of this territory at one time or another. Russia and Spain were willing to turn their claims over to the United States, leaving the Oregon Territory under joint occupation of the United States and England. Settlers poured into Oregon via the Oregon Trail during the early 1840s. This led to a treaty with England in 1846 giving all land below the forty-ninth parallel to the United States. Settlement of this area was slower than in California. Consequently, what is today Oregon and Washington remained frontier until the latter half of the nineteenth century.

The final American frontier was the land left unexplored, unsettled, and undeveloped between the Rocky Mountains and roughly the ninety-eighth meridian. This area was part of the Louisiana Purchase and remained a frontier from 1803, when it was first obtained, to roughly 1900. Known as the Intermountain Frontier, this area required a number of circumstances before settlement could be realized. One was the steady discovery of gold and silver from 1858 through the 1870s, which encouraged people to mine and settle in what is today Nevada, Colorado, Montana, Idaho, and the Black Hills. These frontiers developed quickly because the large influx of miners and others created a booming population growth. Improved transportation as well as modernized mining techniques promoted this rapid population increase. Statehood for these areas came as early as 1864 for Nevada and was complete by 1890.

An influx of religious colonizers in Utah (Mormons) during the 1850s and 1860s promoted settlement in that frontier area. In North and South Dakota and Wyoming, improved train transportation promoted the settlement of that portion of the frontier by ranchers and farmers during the 1870s and 1880s. Oklahoma, which had been set aside as an Indian reservation as early as 1825, finally gave in to the governmental pressure created by people wishing to settle this land for farming and ranching. A series of land rushes beginning in 1889 and continuing until 1895 brought large numbers of people into that frontier. In New Mexico and Arizona the lure of gold first brought a wave of miners in 1858 and then again in 1862. The arid climate, which was poor for farming and ranching, discouraged further settlement and slowed the process. It was not until irrigation techniques were improved and transportation became available that the frontier, made up of New Mexico and Arizona, came to an end. Statehood was not realized for both until 1912.

Settlement of the Intermountain Frontier was delayed by the difficult environment it posed the settler. Once the technology and transportation improved, however, settlement came more rapidly here than in any of the other frontiers. Roughly 140 years were needed to settle all the frontier from the Piedmont to the Mississippi River, whereas the Western Frontier—nearly twice that size—was settled inside of 80 years.

Purpose:

Students will visualize the five different frontiers, their boundaries, and the states they eventually became by mapping them.

Procedure:

1. Reproduce and hand out copies of the instructions, frontier information, and maps to all students (pages 6, 7, and 8).

2. In developing the frontier map, students will need to use the physical land features that are provided to outline the frontier areas. Students can decide to use color or line symbols to denote the different frontier areas. Be certain students include keys at the bottom of their maps for their symbols.

3. Each state is outlined so that students can label it. This will enable students to see what states were created from each frontier area. Encourage students to use other maps to help them with this project.

4. Finally, students label all land and water features and add others that they imagine affected pioneer movement. For example, students will label the Missouri River, but they can use other atlases to locate, add, and label the Arkansas River, which would have been both a barrier and an aid to pioneer travel.

5. Students may work in pairs or small cooperative groups of three when designing the map.

6. Below is an answer key for this activity.

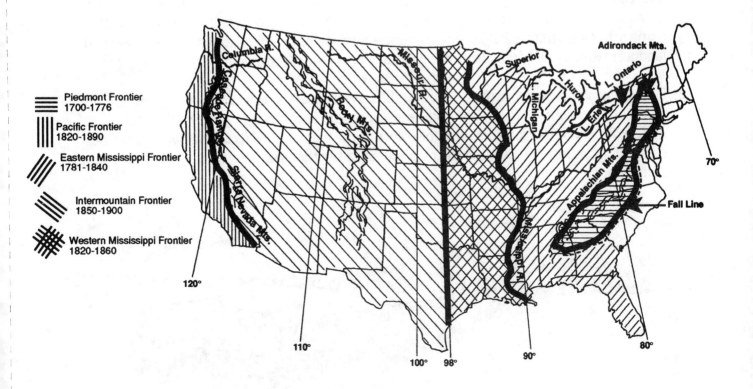

Name_____

Mapping the Frontiers

The American frontier was really five different frontier areas. They were the Piedmont, the Eastern Mississippi Frontier, the Western Mississippi Frontier, the Pacific Frontier, and the Intermountain Frontier. Natural barriers, such as mountain ranges, fall lines, and rivers, created these frontiers. These barriers had to be overcome before each frontier could be opened by settlers.

One might believe that these frontiers were settled one at a time but that was not always the case. The Piedmont, Eastern Mississippi Region, and Western Mississippi Frontier were settled one after another. The Pacific Frontier, however, was being settled at the same time as the Eastern and Western Mississippi Frontiers. The Intermountain Frontier was opened only after the others had been settled.

Instructions:

1. You are to use the map to draw the boundary lines of the five frontier areas. Create a dark line for each boundary.

2. Label each frontier area and its dates of settlement.

3. Using other maps as resources, label each state. This will allow you to see which states were formed from each frontier.

4. Using other resources, label all land and water formations on the map. Add other rivers and land formations that you believe may have affected pioneer expansion.

5. Denote each area by line symbols or color. Line symbols are a series of parallel lines that go in different directions—\\\\ or //// or ||||. These lines should be drawn in pencil lightly but noticeably. If you use color, select light colors or use colored pencils so that writing beneath each color can be seen. Beneath the map include a key that indicates what symbol goes with each frontier.

Mapping the Frontiers

Frontier Information

1. Piedmont—This frontier started at the fall line of the Appalachian Mountains and continued west to the crest of those mountains. To the north it began in the Adirondack Mountains and ended in northwest Georgia. Settlement of the Piedmont began around 1700 and was established by the beginning of the American Revolution in 1776.

2. Eastern Mississippi Frontier—This frontier began at the crest of the Appalachians and extended to the Mississippi River. The entire Mississippi River formed its western boundary. Although the French had set up forts as early as the seventeenth century, serious settlement did not begin until after the Revolutionary War, 1781. By 1840 it was no longer considered a frontier.

3. Western Mississippi Frontier—Beginning at the Mississippi River, this frontier extended west to about the ninety-eighth meridian (98° longitude). It is at this point that the climate became too dry for pioneers to farm successfully with the technology that was available to them. This area was part of the Louisiana Purchase of 1803. Settlement began in the 1820s and lasted until the 1860s.

4. Pacific Frontier—The Pacific Ocean is the western boundary of this frontier. From that coast it extends eastward to the Cascade Range in the north and the Sierra Nevada Range in the south. The crests of those ranges would make up the eastern boundary. Spaniards first explored and settled parts of this frontier as early as the eighteenth century. Both England and the United States also claimed joint ownership to the Oregon Territory in 1818. Beginning in the 1820s settlers began moving into the Pacific frontier. The United States gained possession of the entire frontier by 1848 just in time for the gold rush of 1849. By 1890 the entire coastal area had achieved statehood.

5. Intermountain Frontier—This final frontier was assaulted by settlers from both the east and the west. This immense area extended from the ninety-eighth meridian in the east to the crest of the Cascade and Sierra Nevada ranges in the west. It was the largest frontier area. Miners moved in from the west looking for gold and silver beginning in the 1850s. Later, ranchers and farmers invaded from the east gaining land for cattle and crops. By the end of the nineteenth century, this huge area was no longer considered a frontier.

CHAPTER TWO
The Pioneer

Describing the American Pioneer

Television, films, and novels have romanticized the American pioneer to the point of legend. *Noble, resourceful, industrious, courageous, wise, sober,* and *self-sufficient* are all words that have been assigned to the men and women who heroically opened new land. This idealized version of the pioneer would most likely not contain a list of descriptives like *illiterate, crude, lazy, stubborn,* or *anti-social.* The reality of the American pioneers is that they were all of the above and more. In addition, we may also describe these people as self-reliant, keen-eyed, intolerant, foul-mouthed, superstitious, and belligerent. How could one group of people who share such a similar set of circumstances contain such conflicting character traits? The answer lies in our understanding that the American pioneer who trailblazed the new frontier and was given to raucous behavior was most certainly not the same American pioneer who bought and improved farms, supported subscription libraries, and valued both education and fair play. Students will begin to understand what kind of people the American pioneers were when they understand the three successive waves of pioneers that entered the frontier.

ACTIVITY *Describing the American Pioneer*

The following activity is best used as an introduction prior to instruction. It will get students to realize what their notions of the American pioneer are and consider how they developed them.

Purpose:
Students will construct a written and visual picture of how they believe the American pioneer looked and acted.

Procedure:
1. Duplicate and distribute the activity sheet entitled "Portrait of a Pioneer." Students should fill it out individually.

2. Based on their selections, students develop a paragraph or two that describes the person they have designed by their choices. The paragraph(s) can include both a physical description of the person and a discussion of his character traits.

   Variation—This paragraph can be made into a narrative by telling students to write from the point of view of a traveler who had just met the person.

3. Option—Have students add an illustration of the person they wrote about. The illustration can be hand drawn, but few students usually have that kind of talent or confidence. Allow them to look through magazines and cut out a picture of a person they think best fits their description even if it is a picture of a person in a modern setting. Some students may want to photocopy an illustration from a book.

4. Allow students to share their ideas first in groups of four or five. In addition to having them share their paragraphs, have them each tell the group how they came by these ideas. (For example, is this a composite of movies they have seen or stories they have read?)

5. As a class, discuss some of the ideas brought out in the groups.

Note—The finished character sketches with illustrations make a great bulletin board.

Portrait of a Pioneer

Ask any five people how the American pioneer looked and acted and you are likely to get five different opinions. In the last century even historians have disagreed over who this person really was.

You will find 11 sets of choices below and on the next page. Each set has three possibilities. Choose the *one* in each set that you believe best describes what you imagine the American pioneer to be like.

The American pioneer was most likely

_____ male.
_____ female.
_____ male or female.

The American pioneer made his living as

_____ a hunter/trapper.
_____ a farmer.
_____ a rancher.

The American pioneer most likely

_____ had a family that came with him/her west.
_____ was a loner.
_____ had a family back East.

The American pioneer

_____ explored new land.
_____ farmed new land.
_____ improved on land cleared by others.

In the face of danger the American pioneer probably first considered

_____ himself or herself.
_____ his or her family.
_____ his or her horse.

The American pioneer

_____ was educated.
_____ could read very little and only write his/her name.
_____ was completely illiterate.

Regarding morals and ethics, the American pioneer

_____ was a cheat and liar who took advantage of others.
_____ was an honest, God-fearing person.
_____ went to church and acted self-righteous but was not above doing whatever was
necessary to get ahead.

The American pioneer wore

_____ clothes made in the East.
_____ clothes made out of cloth he or she wove and stitched.
_____ clothes made out of animal hide like buckskin and raccoon hats.

With respect to cleanliness, the American pioneer

_____ was unbelievably filthy and smelled like it.
_____ believed cleanliness was next to Godliness and acted so.
_____ bathed once a week and washed up daily.

With respect to family background, the American pioneer

_____ came from a poor family and was looking for a better life.
_____ was a fugitive from the law.
_____ came from a well-to-do family and was hoping to become independently wealthy.

During his/her lifetime the American pioneer

_____ lived in one location, which he or she passed on to heirs.
_____ lived in several places, selling each one to someone else.
_____ never settled down.

The First Wave

The first people to invade a new frontier were the hunters and trappers. Men dominated this group. They were the individualists who provided the model of the American pioneer as a self-reliant trailblazer. Daniel Boone epitomizes the romanticized notion of this type of pioneer. Daniel Boone, however, does not typify the average first-wave frontiersman. At least one-third were illiterate. Some were lawbreakers using the deep frontier as their way of escaping deeds done to society. Many were foul-mouthed braggarts who prided themselves on their abilities to drink and to fight.

The pioneers' relations with native Americans were mixed. Some established respectable relations with tribes. They honored the hunting grounds and traded goods with the tribes for furs. The French most notably behaved in this manner because hunting and trapping were their primary businesses. Other pioneers were less kind in their dealings. They cheated the native Americans, went back on their word, invaded their hunting grounds, and indiscriminately killed men, women, and children. Needless to say, it was this second variety of hunter/trapper that laid the groundwork of what became a struggle between the two cultures.

The first-wave pioneers were semi-nomadic. They threw up crude shelters, usually three-sided lean-tos, and moved on when the game became scarce or when civilization got too close. They did nothing to improve the land, at least not intentionally. They wore buckskin clothing that they made themselves and ate what they trapped or shot. Entertainment was scarce since they were so detached from civilization. Many were loners and did not seek ties with family or friends. They could be raucous and crude, especially when they had too much to drink, which was probably their most popular form of entertainment. Their aversion to regular hygiene left them infested with fleas and body lice. Because these men were often the first that native Americans encountered, it is no wonder that Indians considered all white men to be a dirty and crude race.

These first-wave pioneers were consistently the openers of each frontier area. In addition to trading their furs, they acted as guides for the people who eventually sought to establish farms in the frontier. In that respect, they played a vital role in the westward expansion of our country. In most cases they hunted and trapped. In a few of the frontier areas they were miners (as in the case of the Pacific and Intermountain Frontiers). They provided useful information regarding the lay of the land, navigable waterways, hostile tribes, and trails through mountains.

The Second Wave—Squatters

Poor is the single word that best describes the second-wave pioneer. The people that sought to escape impoverished conditions in the East saw the American frontier as their way to a better life. In the eighteenth century the standard of primogeniture (i.e., the right of the first-born son to inherit the entire family estate) forced many second- and third-born to seek their life westward. Historically, the South had become populated by a number of indentured servants who, after working for freedom, had settled small farms that produced little of a livelihood due to poor farming practices or outright laziness. Their sons and daughters became part of this second wave as trappers reported Eden-like conditions out West.

Because these people had little or no money to begin with, the prospect of free or inexpensive land was a tremendous lure. Often, the man made his way into the frontier to establish a claim. Then he would return to get his family. Sometimes the entire family went westward together. The government set up land offices that allowed people to put in claims. Land was cheap as long as a person agreed to stay put and improve it. Nonetheless, many of these second-wave settlers did not have the patience or the temperament to put up with organized land regulations and thus simply set up their cabins, becoming known as *squatters*. When another settler came along that did take the time to register and pay for the land, the squatter often sold his improvements and moved on to the edge of another frontier.

The squatter was little more educated than his predecessor, the trapper. He was not much cleaner in life style either and held many superstitious beliefs regarding health and medicine. In demeanor he could be foul-mouthed and belligerent. He saw the land as his for the taking and ignored any treaties that may have been established with native tribes. Consequently, relations between native Americans and whites only deteriorated further as a result of the squatters' presence.

The squatter was a bad farmer when he lived in the East and employed the same land-depleting practices when he reached the frontier. Consequently, it was not uncommon for this first settler to move on to another patch of land several times. Squatters made the initial clearing of the land and lived in cabins made of notched logs. Each generally owned a cow, a mule or horse, and some pigs. Farming was merely at a subsistence level and corn was the main crop. Hunting still provided an important means of getting food.

The West did provide a new social situation for these second-wave pioneers, equality. It took long hard hours to clear and set up a cabin and then maintain it. Everyone in the family worked. Back East there may have been a social stratification, but here everyone was equal in their effort to survive. This concept of frontier equality is one of the notions that later shaped today's view of social class.

The Third Wave—Settlers

Once land had been explored and initially improved, the third-wave pioneers arrived. They were often the buyers of the second-wave person's farms. They were better off financially from the start. Some were even land speculators who could afford to wait and see if a territory, as it developed, was promising as an investment. Some were looking to get out from under the overcrowding conditions of the East. They brought with them the tools, the knowledge, and the animals to properly develop the farm, and they stayed permanently. Many of their descendants may still own the land today.

In addition to permanent improvement, these third-wave settlers brought civilization to the frontier. Crude settlements became towns, and law and order was established that exceeded the personal form of justice that the first- and second-wave pioneers may have handed out. Most of all, the third wavers brought religion, almost always Christian in nature. Whether it was Methodist, Presbyterian, Baptist, or Congregationalist, religion tempered the wild nature of the West.

The third-wave pioneers were much more civilized in their demeanor. Church on Sunday forced them to bathe more regularly. The fact that they were living on land and in settlements that were considerably more improved also resulted in healthier living conditions. Transportation and communication with the East allowed for a higher standard of living, regardless of which frontier they inhabited. They not only tended to be better educated than their predecessors, but they also valued education enough to pass it on to their children by establishing schools.

They grew enough food to live on and then planted enough to be sold. Thus, the farms of the third-wave pioneer were established for their cash crops. In the Pacific frontier where mining was the spark that triggered settlement, men and women established businesses to service the mining populations. In the Intermountain Frontier, men and women of the third wave created businesses to service the cattle ranchers. Towns grew around these businesses, and thus, civilization was established.

All Three Waves Were Pioneers

Students will have an easy time understanding the concept of three waves of pioneers. It is important, however, that they also understand that some men and women moved from one wave to another. A family could come out West as part of the second wave and construct a crude sod house, then stay and improve the land permanently by building a wooden home, becoming part of the civilization and settlements that eventually sprang up around them. Students should also understand that these three waves of American pioneers do not neatly include other people who contributed to the establishment of the frontier. People like riverboat men, soldiers who fought in the Indian wars, and women who specifically came out West to marry widowers make the lines that separate the three waves rather hazy. It was a dynamic process, the civilization of the frontier, but the pattern of trapper, squatter, and settler was one repeated over and over again as the frontier changed.

In discussing the American pioneer with students, it should also be pointed out that all three waves were necessary parts of the opening of each frontier. The trappers and squatters may have been coarse in their demeanor, but their self-reliance and long-suffering attitude cleared the way for civilization. They made agriculture possible and were really on the cutting edge of civilization. The third wave actually civilized the West. They made permanent improvements on the land, created permanent settlements, and developed the elements of justice, education, and religion for the frontier.

ACTIVITY *Pioneer Biographies*

After students have had a chance to note the development of the three waves of pioneers, the following activity will give them the opportunity to use that information. The biographies presented on the following page are fictitious but realistic. They are composites of people that really lived.

Purpose:

To analyze and interpret biographical information to determine in what wave of American pioneer each subject would belong.

Procedure:

1. Duplicate and distribute copies of the biographical sketches from the page entitled "Pioneer Biographies."

2. Have students read each biography and determine to which of the three waves of American pioneers the subject belongs. Since none of the subjects clearly fits in any one wave, you may want to have students identify which information places the subject in each wave. This can be done by having students create a chart on which they separate the information. They then use the chart to make a final decision. This step should be done individually.

3. Pair students or put them in small groups with the instructions that they must reach consensus regarding in which wave each subject was placed.

4. Lead a full class discussion about their team decisions. You may want to chart the teams' results and tabulate their decisions.

   Note—There are no definite answers for each biographical subject. The emphasis is on how students analyze and interpret the data and what criteria they develop in their decision making.

5. As a follow-up, have students develop their own biographical sketches and share them with the class.

Pioneer Biographies

Directions:

Below are three biographical sketches of American pioneers. Although these people never existed, the sketches are realistic. You are to read each one and determine in which wave of pioneers each would belong. Be prepared to defend your decision.

Strategy:

Since the biographical sketches you will read contain information that could place the person in two or three different pioneer waves, you may need to separate the information. One way is to make a quick chart that allows you to separate the information according to which wave of American pioneers it fits.

1. Ben McGee

Ben McGee came to Kentucky (it was then part of Virginia) when he learned from his brother that life was grand in this land west of the Appalachian Mountains. Although he was due to inherit his father's farm in North Carolina, the prospect of better land interested him. So he left his parents and arranged to meet with his brother at Boone's Fort. When he arrived, he found out that his brother had been killed in an Indian raid. He stayed at the fort for awhile. During that time some trappers arrived with dozens of pelts. This convinced Ben that he would be better off trapping than farming. He sold everything he had and set out gathering beaver, mink, fox, and ermine furs, trading them for what he needed. This he did alone for 10 years. During this time he married a woman from the Shawnee tribe, and together they set up a cabin and lived south of the Ohio River. Ben continued to gather pelts, however, using them to trade for the things his family needed. When he died, his wife and family moved back with the Shawnee.

Pioneer Biographies

2. Amelia Whitting

Amelia lived in Maine. She married a fisherman who was lost at sea during her second year of marriage. In a newspaper she read a personal ad from Marcus Whitting who was seeking a wife to live with him and help raise his two sons in the Nebraska Territory. Marcus was widowed, too. Amelia traveled out West, met Marcus, and decided to marry him. They lived in a sod house and endured many hardships, including tornadoes and locusts. They planted wheat, had some cows and chickens, and basically got by on what they grew. After seven years of marriage, a small town called Brownlee sprang up. When a typhoid epidemic spread through the town, Marcus became infected and died. Amelia decided to stick it out. Eventually, her two step-sons imported some lumber and built a wooden home. Three years before Amelia died at the age of 59, Nebraska became a state.

3. "Gold Pan" Smith

Jimmy Smith was born in the Oregon Territory in 1828. He worked his parents' farm until he heard about the gold discovery in California in 1849. Jimmy left home to make his fortune roaming the unmapped mountains of California looking for gold. He did become rich but not by finding gold. Although Jim did do some prospecting, he found that he could make more money selling tin pans to the men who came to strike it rich. This he did with great success. He turned his business into a string of general stores throughout the California mining regions and by the age of 33 was one of the richest men in California. After the Civil War, Jimmy decided to invest in land in the Wyoming Territory because he heard that silver and gold were being mined from the mountains. He sold his general stores and at the age of 44 bought thousands of acres of land hoping to strike it rich. He hired miners and brought in heavy equipment. Small towns sprouted where his mines were working. All of the mines, however, were unsuccessful. Within seven years the towns and the mines were deserted. Jimmy died alone—a poor man panning for gold.

CHAPTER THREE
The Roads West

Overcoming the Great Barrier

What the Atlantic Ocean was to the first explorers, the Appalachian Mountains were to the pioneers. During the seventeenth century Virginia colonists began expanding westward. Their first barrier was the fall line. This imaginary line that links the waterfalls of the rivers flowing east from the Appalachian Mountains halted the easy advancement of settlers who were using the navigable waterways of these rivers. As the population increased, however, portaging the rivers was accomplished, and the Piedmont slowly became inhabited. By 1725 settlers occupied many of the valleys east of the Appalachian ridge and west of the fall line. These mountains became known as the Great Barrier, and they (along with the Indians) prevented further westward expansion. Consequently, the settlers spread southward drifting into what is today North Carolina. What was lacking for pioneers to move beyond the Great Barrier were trails.

From Trail to Turnpike

As early as the 1750s roads were being constructed westward. The circumstances surrounding the development of these roads were not always in keeping with a frontier spirit, however. Braddock's Road, for example, was constructed by General Braddock's army in 1755 during the French and Indian War as it marched toward Fort Duquesne in a disastrous effort to take that fort. General Braddock lost his life in the battle but the road kept his name. It extended from Fort Cumberland (present day Cumberland) almost to the Ohio River.

In 1758 General John Forbes struck out toward Fort Duquesne hoping to succeed where Braddock had failed. He did. In the process he created what became known as Forbes Road. It began at Harris' Ferry (present-day Harrisburg). Both of these roads, although originally of military importance, became main arteries for westward travelers. New Englanders used Forbes Road, while the Southern settlers relied on Braddock's Road to get them over the Great Barrier to the Ohio River. From there they could float down the Ohio on rafts to any one of a number of settlements along that river.

Both roads fell into disrepair, and had it not been for the push of people trying to get out West they might have become a trivia question on some graduate professor's exam. Instead, both roads developed into key factors of westward expansion. After the Revolutionary War Ebenezer Zane blazed a *trace* (or trail) leading from Limestone, Kentucky (today Maysville) to Wheeling, Virginia (today West Virginia). In 1796 he opened this up to wagon traffic. The influx of settlers was so great that old Braddock's Road became literally choked with traffic. This prompted Congress, after a great amount of squabbling, to appropriate money for a National Road that led from Baltimore through Cumberland along Braddock's Road to Wheeling by 1818. In time, the National Road extended all the way to Columbus, Ohio and beyond to Indianapolis, Indiana and Vandalia, Illinois. Thus, what was once just a weed-choked army road in the 1760s turned into one of the first national highways ushering in thousands of pioneers from the East.

Forbes Road's evolution is no less amazing. By 1783 northern emigrants from Massachusetts, Connecticut, New Jersey, and New York were calling it the Pennsylvania Road. The traffic on this road grew and demanded improvement upon improvement until today travelers on the scenic Pennsylvania Turnpike follow the same general trail that settlers did over 200 years ago.

The Wilderness Trail

One of the most famous early westward routes was the Wilderness Trail. As pioneers settled in the eastern valleys of the Appalachian Mountains, a route developed that could take settlers diagonally across Virginia in the shadow of the Appalachian crest. This valley route extended from Fredericktown through Winchester in northern Virginia. It continued southwest through the eastern valleys of the Appalachian Mountains to Wythe (today Wytheville) in southern Virginia. From there it wound its way over the mountains into present-day Tennessee and Fort Watauga. This settlement was established in 1769 along the Watauga River. It's significance is that it was located on the other side of the divide. It was from here that many a pioneer set off into the land of "canes and turkeys," known today as Kentucky. (Cane was a type of grass valued by early pioneers that was found throughout the Southeast.)

As the Revolutionary War was getting started in the East, a man who was to become a legend in the Old West began to blaze his trail into Kentucky. Daniel Boone was hired by Judge Richard Henderson to create a trail leading into the territory he had purchased from the Cherokees. (His illegal Transylvania Company eventually had to give up all claims to this land.) Starting from Fort Watauga, Boone and 40 men traveled to the extreme southwest end of Virginia and crossed through the Cumberland Gap. From here they turned directly north and followed a trail used by the native Americans known as the Warriors Path. Once across the Cumberland River, they headed northwest following a trace created by woodland buffalo. These traces were quite visible and noticeably wide in some places. They helped lead Boone and his troupe to a location on the Kentucky River just southeast of present-day Lexington, Kentucky. There Boone built a blockhouse and today the town is still known as Boonesborough.

Interestingly, Boone was not the first to enter this territory and establish a settlement. A year earlier in 1774, James Harrod had established a fort west and a little south of Boone's location. Fort Harrod eventually became known as Harrodsburg which still exists today. Settlers wishing to get to Fort Harrod would follow the Wilderness Trail and the branch off farther northwest in the area that is today Madison County, Kentucky.

The Water Trails

The Ohio River provided a natural and necessary transportation system for any pioneer interested in heading West. This was especially true because of the slow pace at which the National Road was built. It took until 1818 to complete the road as far as Wheeling. It took until 1833 to get as far as Columbus, Ohio and four more years before it reached the western border of Ohio.

Most settlers using the Ohio River came from the Northeast. They used the Forbes Road and traveled as far as Redstone Old Fort (eventually named Brownsville), located on the Monongahela River south of Fort Pitt (Pittsburgh). Some made it as far as Pittsburgh. At either location, they built or bought a flatboat to float down the Ohio River. The best times for travel were spring and late fall since melting snow or rains put the river level high enough to avoid rapids, sandbars, snags, and other problems. In time, Wheeling, Virginia (today West Virginia) developed as another popular embarkation point.

In the first quarter century of the 1800s, there were many popular stopping points along the Ohio River which acted as settlement points or gateways to new land. Steubenville, Ohio, whose population was 800 by 1812, provided supplies for the area's farms. Settlers also stopped at Marietta, Ohio, which became a shipbuilding center floating its product down the Ohio to the Mississippi and the Gulf of Mexico. Point Pleasant, Virginia (now West Virginia) acted as a gateway south into the valley between the Great and Little Kanawah Rivers. Many pioneers got off at Limestone (today Maysville) where nearby Zane's Trace led them into Ohio. In fact, Zane's Trace went through Chillicothe. The land between Chillicothe and Cincinnati was fertile for wheat, and the tributaries of the Ohio aided its shipment.

If settlers wished to travel even farther west, they tended to get off at Louisville, Kentucky. This is the part of the Ohio River where the falls are located, and the risk of completely losing the raft and its belongings was greatest. On the opposite shore of Louisville was Jeffersonville. A buffalo trace could be picked up here and settlers could take it all the way to Vincennes. Vincennes was an old French settlement on the Wabash River that had gradually become an American town. Along this trace pioneers fanned out establishing farming communities along the way.

Going West in the North

Main arteries west took settlers along the southern portion of Ohio, Indiana, and Illinois. Consequently, these were the first to develop. Farther to the north the route that settlers followed was the only route that crossed no mountains. To get to the area known as the Western Reserve (northeastern Ohio) and beyond, settlers relied on the water travel afforded by the Great Lakes. Pioneers seeking land in this area were mostly New Englanders. The typical route had them following the Hudson River north and then heading west along the Mohawk river. From there they used the Genessee Road through Oneida and the Genessee Valley to Buffalo and Lake Erie. Ships could be boarded at that point taking settlers to Cleveland and Detroit. By 1818 steamboat travel was launched on Lake Erie carrying over 200 passengers and their belongings to their destination within 10 days. West of Lake Erie the Maumee river could be followed as far as Ft. Wayne. Beyond that the Wabash River transported settlers south and west to the Ohio River and then to the Mississippi.

Going West in the South

In the North the frontier expanded westward at a steady rate. As a pioneer moved west, he expected conditions to grow more and more primitive. This was not true in the south. Along the Mississippi a few settlements developed early. Both New Orleans and Natchez can trace their origin to the first quarter of the 1700s. These towns provided commerce centers for goods traveling south to the Gulf of Mexico. They attracted rivermen and ruffians but not the family settlers found up North. The only real trail that existed from the Mississippi eastward was the Natchez trace. It served as a return route for men shipping goods down the Mississippi. It stretched between Natchez, Mississippi and Nashville, Tennessee. When steamboat travel finally became a reality in the second decade of the 1800s, settlements began to spread along the Mississippi River.

No major trails or waterways linked the Mississippi River with the developed cities of the South such as Charleston. In addition, the Cherokees, Creeks, Seminoles, Chickasaws, and Choctaws (known as the five civilized tribes) all held land rights that they refused to give up. The federal government finally forced them out between 1816 and 1840. Consequently, most of Alabama and Mississippi remained a wilderness to settlers until the 1820s. During that decade plantations began to flourish and in the following decade towns and villages sprang up in support of them.

ACTIVITY *Trails West*

Hearing or reading about the trails does not give students enough of an understanding of how these trails were planned by the pioneers. Any travel route had to be relatively safe and if the distances were great enough the route had to supply food and water. Consequently, many routes skirted rivers and lakes, following traces of animals and avoided wherever possible mountains and river crossings.

Purpose:

To allow students to visualize the routes that American pioneers used to travel west. To allow students to evaluate these routes and suggest alternate routes.

Procedure:

1. Hand out copies of "Trails West I" and "Map the Trails."

2. Using the directions given on the "Trails West I" sheet, have students draw and label each route.

   It is impossible to exactly map each route and trail. This is especially true with the Natchez Trace. Allow students to notice differences in their maps and discuss whether these differences would have any effect on the traveler.

3. A similar activity is presented further into the unit entitled "Trails West II." Students follow the same procedures for a map dealing with the trails leading from the Mississippi River to the Pacific Ocean.

4. Hindsight is always 20-20. Have students look over the map of trails after they are finished and have them try to design a better or alternate trail West.

5. All the trails headed west. None of them went north. Why, for example, weren't trails developed running north to the Dakotas? Why wasn't western Texas or Nebraska pursued as much as Oregon? The answer to these questions can be found by looking closely at the geography of these areas. Have students research these states and then speculate as to why settlers did not choose to develop them.

Name _____

Trails West I

Introduction:

Movement westward for the pioneer involved planning the route to take. In some cases there was no decision since there was only one possible route. In the end a network of roads and waterways was created that connected the eastern U.S. to the Mississippi River. Using the directions given below, draw and label each route that settlers used to move westward.

Directions:

1. *Forbes Road*—Begin at Harris' Ferry. Go southwest through Carlisle and Shippensburg to Fort Loudon. Change direction and head northwest directly to Fort Pitt.

2. *Braddock's Road*—Begin at Baltimore. Travel west through Frederickstown to Hagerstown. At Hagerstown begin skirting the Potomac River to Old Town. Turn northwest at Old Town and pass Fort Necessity on your way to Fort Pitt.

3. *The Wilderness Trail*—Begin at Frederickstown and head southwest along the east side of the Appalachian Mountains. Travel through Winchester to Wythe. At Wythe pick up the Holston River and follow it until you need to turn south to arrive at Watauga. From Watauga head due west and pass through the Cumberland Gap. Head directly north after passing through the gap and head northwest to Boone's Fort or turn west and go to Fort Harrod.

4. *Zane's Trace*—Begin at Limestone and travel northeast to Chillicothe. At Chillicothe begin heading east until you can cross the Muskingum River due west of Wheeling. Travel east to Wheeling.

5. *The Northern Route*—Begin in New York City. Follow the Hudson River north to the Mohawk River. Travel west following the Mohawk to Ft. Stanwix. From Ft. Stanwix reach Lake Oneida and follow its northern shore and the north bank of the Seneca River westward. At Seneca Lake head due west past the Genessee River to Buffalo. At Buffalo take a boat that will travel to Cleveland and Detroit via Lake Erie.

6. *The Natchez Trace*—Begin in Natchez and travel to the westernmost point of the Pearl River. Turn north toward Big Black River and follow it until it ends. Continue heading north and east and cross the Tombigbee River, the Tennessee River, and the Duck River until you get to Nashville.

Filling in the Map

Below are some additional historical and current items to include on your map. The section entitled "A Complete Pioneer Map" will help to give you a more accurate view of what the Old West looked like to the settler. If you complete the section entitled "Today's Map" you will be able to see where some of today's cities and landmarks would have existed 200 years ago.

A Complete Pioneer Map

1. Waterways were main routes used by many pioneers. Trace over the Ohio River from its source at Fort Pitt to its mouth at the Mississippi.

2. Use an atlas to locate the following cities on the Ohio River which were a part of the early history of Ohio, Virginia, and Kentucky: Wheeling, Steubenville, Marietta, Point Pleasant, Limestone (Maysville), Cincinnati, Louisville.

3. Use an atlas to locate and draw these rivers on the map:
    In Ohio—Miami River and Maumee River,
    In Pennsylvania—Susquehanna River and Allegheny River
    In Indiana—Wabash River
    In Kentucky and Tennessee—Kentucky River, Cumberland River

4. The National Road was finally completed in 1852. By then it had been made obsolete by canals and railroads. Draw the National Road by linking the following cities. The date next to each city is the date in which the road reached that city.
    Baltimore—starting point
    Cumberland—1810
    Wheeling—1818 (follow Forbes Road)
    Columbus—1833 (the Erie Canal was already operating)
    Indianapolis—1842 (approximately)
    Vandalia—1852

Today's Map

5. Lightly draw in the outlines of each of the following states: New York, Pennsylvania, Maryland, Virginia, West Virginia, Ohio, Kentucky, Indiana, Illinois, Mississippi, Tennessee, Alabama, North Carolina, South Carolina, Georgia.

6. Many cities have developed along what was once a trail or around what was once a fort or a small village. Use an atlas and label prominent cities whose growth may have been influenced by the movement and settling of pioneers.

Map the Trails I

1. Baltimore
2. Fredericktown
3. Hagerstown
4. Old Town
5. Ft. Necessity
6. Ft. Pitt
7. Harris Ferry
8. Carlisle/Shippensburg
9. Ft. Loudon
10. Winchester
11. Wythe
12. Fort Watauga
13. Cumberland Gap

14. Boone's Fort
15. Ft. Harrod
16. Limestone
17. Chillicothe
18. Wheeling
19. New York City
20. Ft. Stanwix
21. Lake Oneida
22. Buffalo
23. Cleveland
24. Detroit
25. Natchez
26. Nashville

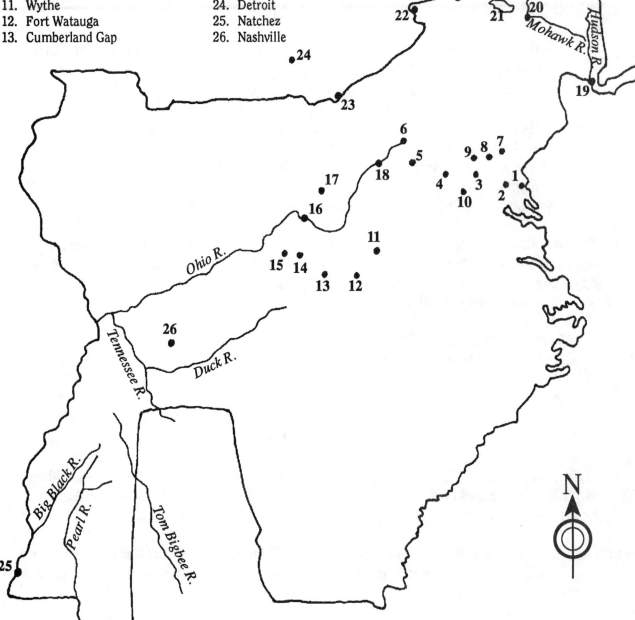

Beyond the Mississippi

For all the roads, routes, and waterways that existed east of the Mississippi, one would think that there would be a great many more in the expanse of land west of the Mississippi. Surprisingly, there were only three or four routes that were regularly used by the pioneers heading west across the prairie and mountains. These are the Santa Fe Trail, the Oregon Trail, the California Trail, and the Mormon Trail. Many other trails existed but served other purposes. For example, the Pony Express route was a mail route, and the Chisolm trail was used for cattle drives.

The year 1821 was a good year for the people of the Southwest. That year Mexico became a nation independent of Spain. That year also marked the opening of the Santa Fe Trail. By luck a group of traders met a troup of Spanish-speaking soldiers. Previously, traders who strayed into Spanish territory were jailed, but this time they were directed to the goods-starved Santa Fe. When they returned to Missouri, word quickly spread of the newly opened trade. Within a year caravans were wearing a trail West.

The Santa Fe Trail

The Santa Fe Trail began around Independence, Missouri and headed west to Council Grove, Kansas. Continuing west and south, the trail met up with the Arkansas River and ran alongside it. Near what today is Dodge City, the trail split. One route continued following the Arkansas until it met with the Purgatory River in present-day Colorado near Las Animas. Here was Bent's Fort and the trail turned south skirting the Sangre de Cristos Mountains. From there it turned due west to Santa Fe. The second route was know as the Cimarron Cutoff. It headed southwest directly toward Las Vegas. By following this route a caravan could avoid the hazardous mountains but risked 50 miles of scorching desert.

The Santa Fe Trail was not a true settler's trail. It was used by some who became settlers. It was primarily a trade route and a very lucrative one at that. Its significance lies in the way it caused people to focus their attention on the West as a viable location for settlement. It also helped to create jump-off centers such as Independence, Missouri for other routes west.

The Oregon Trail

The Oregon Trail was easily the most famous of the trails pioneers used to cross the prairie and mountains. Beginning with the Lewis and Clark expedition of 1804, trappers, soldiers, and explorers had blazed their way across the mountains. They found passes, mapped the terrain, noted barriers, and built forts. Each of these steps led to the establishment of the Oregon Trail.

As with the Santa Fe Trail, the Oregon Trail began primarily at Independence, Missouri. Other jumping off points included St. Joseph, Missouri, which was about 50 miles to the north on the Missouri River. Still another was Council Bluffs, Iowa, 125 miles from St. Joseph where the Platte River and the Missouri River converge. All three routes came together along the Platte River in Nebraska at a place called Grand Island.

From there the trail followed the south bank of the Platte River west over the high plains of Nebraska past Scott's Bluff and into Wyoming. Here the trail began its climb into the Rocky Mountains. The first outpost it reached was Fort Laramie (667 miles from Independence). Supplies could be bought (at typical cutthroat prices), wagons repaired, and spirits buttressed during the one- or two-day stay at Fort Laramie.

If the travelers were feeling the least bit discouraged at this point, success would be doubtful because the most hazardous and strenuous portion of the journey was just beginning. From Fort Laramie the trail continued its course along the Platte river past present-day Casper. At the confluence of the Sweetwater and Platte Rivers stood Independence Rock, sometimes called Inscription Rock. It was here that travelers inscribed their names as they headed to South Pass.

The route wound its way over the Continental Divide via the South Pass and then headed south down the Green River to Fort Bridger, near the present-day city of Green River. Here the travelers had another rest to regroup. Jim Bridger had built the fort and sold supplies and entertained the settlers with many of his tall and not-so-tall tales. Jim had spent most of his life as a trapper/trader. Although illiterate, he could speak English, French, Spanish, and several native American dialects. The fort he built in 1843 was in anticipation of the many settlers that he predicted would be traveling west to the Pacific. He was right.

The Oregon Trail (continued)

Now came the hardest part of the trip, 200 miles to Fort Hall. Water was bad, food for the animals was scarce, the trail was rough, and game was difficult to find, let alone shoot. Wagons often broke during this leg and animals could die of heat and thirst. Fort Hall was on the Snake River in Idaho. Today it would be located between the cities of Pocatello and Blackfoot.

The trail continued west and north from Fort Hall toward Fort Boise. Settlers followed the Snake River to get to Fort Boise (present-day Boise, Idaho) but had to abandon the river at this point because of its impassable gorges. Settlers instead followed the Burnt River Valley west and then headed north into a huge valley called Grande Ronde. (Today La Grande, Oregon, is located here.)

Those who were doing well at this point might cross the Blue Mountains, follow the Umatilla River to the Columbia, and finally follow the Columbia River to the Wilmametter River Valley where Fort Vancouver and Oregon City were waiting. On the other hand, if a family's wagon was broken or health was poor they might cross the Blue Mountains taking a more northerly route to a close-by mission on the Walla Walla River. Here they could get their strength back and stock up on supplies before finishing the last leg of the journey down the Columbia.

The entire journey was more than 2,000 miles. Along the way, settlers gave up and returned, died, or even stopped and made a home where they were. Everyone, however, knew when they were done that they had gone as far as they could.

The California Trail

Once the gold bug had bitten some travelers, California became the destination of choice. These travelers followed the Oregon Trail most of the way. Between Fort Bridger and Fort Hall, however, they turned south into what is today Nevada and picked up the Humboldt River. They followed this river to its sink. The route then led them across the desert to the Truckee River (near present-day Reno, Nevada) and up the Sierra Nevada Mountains. It was here that the infamous Donner Party met with tragedy by getting there after the winter snow storms made travel impossible. Once through the pass the trail led through the Central Valley of California toward Sutter's Fort located near present-day Sacramento on the American River.

The Mormon Trail

After facing violent opposition in the Midwest, the followers of the Church of Jesus Christ of the Latter Day Saints, better known as Mormons, set out for Utah Territory, which they believed would be their land of milk and honey. This trail known as the Mormon Trail saw thousands of Mormons cross the prairie and mountains to reach Great Salt Lake. The route itself paralleled the Oregon Trail except that it followed the Platte River on the north bank instead of the south bank. It went past Fort Laramie, and at present-day Casper, Wyoming, the Mormons forded the river and headed through the South Pass to Fort Bridger. From here the trail continued south through the Wasatch Mountains and finally into the Salt Lake Valley.

Trails West II

Introduction:

Settlers moving west away from the Mississippi River had considerably fewer choices of routes than their forefathers who moved west toward the Mississippi. Only four basic routes took settlers toward the west coast, the Santa Fe Trail, the Oregon Trail, the California Trail, and the Mormon Trail. Floating down a river (like the Ohio) was not an option since all rivers east of the Rocky Mountains flowed the wrong way.

Use the directions below to draw each trail and label it.

Directions:

1. *Santa Fe Trail*—Begin at Independence, Missouri. Head west to Council Grove, Kansas. Continue west and south to the Arkansas River and follow the north bank of the river. Follow the river to Bent's Fort. At Bent's Fort cross the river and head south to Las Vegas. At Las Vegas turn west to Santa Fe.

   A cutoff was developed to save time. Near where the Cimarron and Arkansas River come closest, cross the Arkansas River and head straight to Las Vegas. Label this the Cimarron Cutoff.

2. *Oregon Trail*—Begin at Independence or St. Joseph, Missouri or Council Bluffs, Iowa. Head for the Platte River. Follow the south bank of the Platte River to Ft. Laramie. Cross over the Platte to get to Ft. Laramie and then stay on the Platte River to where it meets the Sweetwater River. Follow the Sweetwater River west until it ends and continue west to the South Pass. Go through South Pass and then head south along the Green River to Ft. Bridger. From Ft. Bridger travel west and north to Ft. Hall. At Ft. Hall pick up the Snake River and follow it to Ft. Boise. Head north and west from Ft. Boise past Lone Pine Mountain, past Grande Ronde to the Columbia River. Finally, follow the Columbia River west to Oregon City.

3. *California Trail*—Follow the same directions as the Oregon Trail as far as Ft. Bridger. Between Ft. Bridger turn south and pick up the Humboldt River. Follow this river to its sink across the desert. Pick up the Truckee River and follow it through Donner Pass. Get through the pass and head west and south to Fort Sutter.

4. *Mormon Trail*—Once again use the same directions as the Oregon Trail except follow the Platte River on its north bank. At Fort Bridger head directly southwest across the Wasatch Mountains to the Great Salt Lake.

Map the Trails II

1. Independence
2. Council Grove
3. Bent's Fork
4. Las Vegas
5. Santa Fe
6. St. Joseph
7. Council Bluffs
8. Ft. Laramie
9. South Pass
10. Ft. Bridger
11. Ft. Hall
12. Ft. Boise
13. Lone Pine Mountain
14. Grande Ronde
15. Oregon City
16. Humboldt Sink
17. Donner Pass
18. Sutter's Fort
19. Great Salt Lake

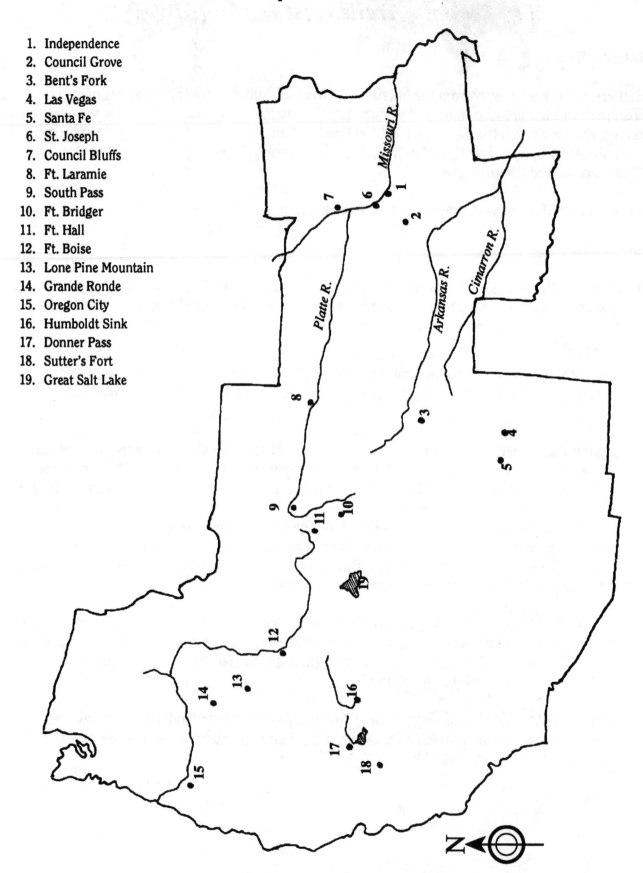

FS-10140 Life as a Pioneer

Map Key for Trails West I and Trails West II

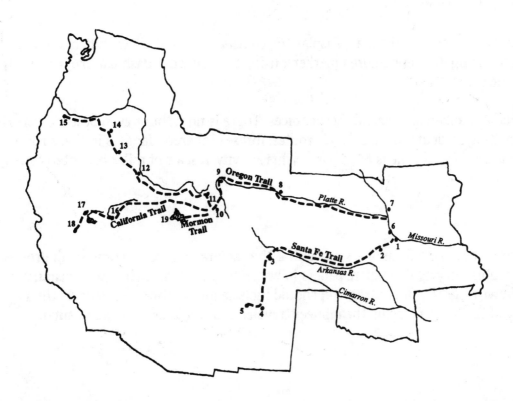

ACTIVITY *Pioneer Decisions*

When traveling West, settlers had to constantly make decisions that would affect their lives. When to leave, what route to take, how much to bring, where to ford a stream, and hundreds of other decisions all resulted in success or failure.

Purpose:

Students will analyze possible pioneer routes to a destination, decide on a best route, and defend their choice.

Procedure:

1. Depending on the class situation, allow students to work in cooperative groups of two or three.

2. Duplicate and distribute copies of "Instructions," "Important Factors," and the map itself. Each group may need two maps, one to be used as a planning map and one as a final copy.

3. Allow students to analyze the map and all possible routes. Have students carefully read the "Important Factors." Each group is to reach a consensus on the best route and be prepared to explain and defend its decisions.

   Note: Students will need help seeing the ramifications of each decision at first. For example, taking an extreme southern route in spring will have them crossing at least three very high rivers due to spring melt runoff. That is a high-risk hazard. If they decide to do it, they have to defend that decision.

4. Prepare a transparency of the map. Display the transparency and allow students to trace their routes using different colored markers, using a specific dot-dash pattern, or simply by labeling the route.

5. Have students explain and defend their choices. There is no right or even best answer. The value is getting students to see possible routes, foresee inherent dangers in these routes, and make decisions. Travel time is not a part of this activity. A scale of miles has intentionally been left out.

Assessment:

This activity could become a form of assessment. Either before or after listening to all groups present their routes, they could prepare papers in which they present their final decisions and defend them in writing. The final paragraph should include information that reflects their understanding of the dangers facing the pioneer traveler and would be assessed as such.

Name _____

Pioneer Decisions—Instructions

Introduction:

Pioneers traveling west undertook a journey that was more hazardous than any we face today when we travel. They were entering a wilderness area that had few signs of civilization. Trails were poorly marked, natural obstructions such as flooded rivers, mountains, and deserts were common. Pioneers had to make decisions that could cost them their lives. The activity you are about to do will allow you to make the same kind of decisions the pioneers made.

Objective:

To plan a route from one of the eastern passes to Settlers Valley in the northwestern end of the land and defend all decisions made in designing that route.

Procedure:

1. Begin by deciding what time of year you will embark on your journey.

2. Choose which pass you will enter, East Pass or South Pass. These are your only two choices.

3. Brainstorm all possible routes.

4. Analyze these routes using the information contained on the "Important Factors" page.

5. Be ready to defend the decisions of your route and explain the reasons for not choosing other routes.

General Information:

1. The purpose of this activity is not to get there first or even prove you could reach Settlers Valley in a set amount of time. The goal is to decide on a best route considering all of the hazards and circumstances.

2. You will be traveling by wagon with a team of slow but dependable oxen and/or floating down a river on a flatboat.

3. If you wish to float down a river at any time you will have to build the flatboat. Make certain you are near a supply of wood.

Pioneer Decisions—Important Factors

1. Spring—The ground is wet and wagons can get stuck. Arrival will be in late summer/early fall.

2. Summer—The ground is dry but by mid-July Invisible Lake is also dry. It will fill again in fall. All rivers are low in summer. This is good for crossing but makes travel on any river impossible. Arrival will be in late fall.

3. Fall—High water levels . . . bad for crossing, good for travel. Arrival will be in winter.

4. America's pioneers usually stuck to well-marked routes to avoid getting lost. They followed rivers and streams, skirted mountain ranges, and used buffalo traces.

5. Buffalo traces are easy routes to follow and easy on the wagons but you risk losing your way in the prairie's desert if you get off of them.

6. Water flows from high to low places. You cannot float upstream. The North River definitely flows east to west.

7. Wagon travel in wooded and mountain areas is very slow-going and hazardous.

8. Water travel is no faster nor slower than land travel.

9. You must portage around waterfalls or rapids.

10. The north bank of the North River is made of sheer cliffs. Any exit or camping or portaging must be on the south side.

11. Because the native tribes have been removed from lands on two other occasions, they are aggressively hostile.

12. Game and water are most plentiful around rivers and lakes. Game is least plentiful in the mountains. Game is harder to find in the prairie desert but available.

13. You only carry enough water at one time for 10 days. It is impossible to get from East Pass to Crystal Lake without several stops for water unless it rains.

14. Salt Lake water is undrinkable. The water flowing into it is miserable but drinkable.

15. Forts are available for restocking supplies.

Pioneer Decisions–Map

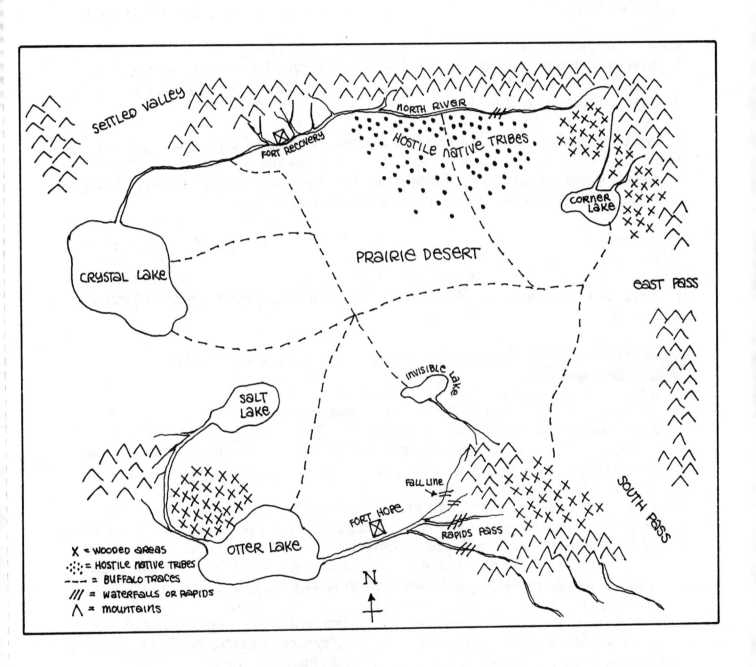

ACTIVITY — *Writing About the Trip*

After students have completed the "Pioneer Decisions" activity they can expand on their experience in a number of ways using creative writing.

1. A Letter Home

Have students imagine that they have arrived at Settlers Valley. Have them prepare a letter to relatives at home that describes some of the hazards encountered.

2. How the Settlers Got There

As a variation, students can include a written description (not a map) of the route they took. The idea is that relatives will use this written description to follow them the next year. Encourage students to forewarn their relatives of dangers and have them include advice they would want to pass along. What, for example, should the relatives bring on the trip?

3. Keep a Diary

Students can keep imaginary diaries of events that took place while on the trip. They can embellish their trip with events, discuss decisions they made to travel one way or another, or include good fortune as well as bad.

ACTIVITY — *Creating a Game*

Students can used the "Pioneer Decisions" map to create their own game. They will need to identify all the possible hazards and rate them according to how dangerous they are. For example, crossing a river in summer has very little danger while trying to travel through mountains has a higher risk.

Once this is done they can transfer these risks into a roll of the dice. For example, for a low-risk hazard a roll of two to six means they made it through the hazard safe. A roll of one means a delay (loss of turn) or death (loss of game). For high-risk hazards a roll of one to five means delay or death and a roll of six means they made it safely. Students can create their own system. Some risks, such as a long desert trek, may involve more than one turn.

Players can then plan a route. As they move along the route, they roll the dice to find out the result of their risk. The first player to reach Settlers Valley wins. It may be possible that no one will. What does that tell them about the real-life risks of America's settlers?

If dice throwing is not preferred, students can make their own spinner with numbers on it and achieve the same result.

CHAPTER FOUR
Transportation West

Getting There Was Slow

Although 100 years separated them, the pioneer of the 1750s and the pioneer of the 1850s had a lot in common with respect to travel. Both were in for a long trip. They had only three sources of transportation available to them—wagons, water, and walking. For the traveling family, wagons were a necessity as a *freight* vehicle for the tons of household goods they would need when they arrived at their destination however, few pioneers relied on a wagon as a *transportation* vehicle. The trip from Missouri to Oregon could be made in four to five months, but few pioneers succeeded in making the trek at such a breakneck pace. Five to six months was the common amount of time. This means the average rate of speed was about 13 miles per day or about 1 or 2 miles per hour. A good day's travel eclipsed 15 miles. The fastest travel occurred on the flat, dry prairie. In the Rocky Mountains and beyond, steep routes and water hazards could stall a wagon train completely.

Water was the easiest, most expensive, and occasionally the most hazardous of the three methods of travel. It was available for travelers in the Old West (east of the Mississippi River) because the rivers flowed westward giving many emigrants the opportunity to float toward their destinations. Time was needed of course to make the raft (10 to 21 days if it were built by one of the professional raft builders, the better part of a year if it were built by the settler himself). The rivers allowed a slow drift with the current that was no faster than land travel but much easier on everyone. The swifter parts of the river were more treacherous and could easily result in a settler losing everything to the bottom of the Ohio River.

By the 1830s canals enabled settlers to move westward from New York to Ohio and via Lake Erie even farther west. Canal systems were further developed in Pennsylvania, Indiana, and Ohio allowing for north-south travel. The rate of transportation was still amazingly slow by our standards (one and one-half miles per hour). The boats tied up at nights and at each lock delays were common because boats were backed up. Still, canal systems cut the travel time by one-third compared to land travel over the mountains in Pennsylvania and New York, so the canal was a great success.

West of the Mississippi River the waterways flowed east, making rafting impossible. Only with the development of the steamboat was upriver travel possible. The first New Orleans-St. Louis round-trip took about 37 days in 1816, but by 1840 the time was cut to five and one-half days. This method of transportation was considerably safer but also more expensive and only gave the far west pioneers a good start.

Of the three, walking was the most reliable and the most common. The early pioneers of the eighteenth century often walked westward with one or two pack animals carrying their possessions. In later years when a family had a wagon and an animal team the bone-jarring ride on the suspensionless wagon made walking a necessary alternative. If oxen were drawing the wagon, someone was needed to walk alongside and act as a guide for these beasts. Consequently, a person could have a wagon but still end up walking nearly the entire way to his or her destination.

Today's highways and cars are light years from what the pioneers faced in their travels. We get aggravated when highway construction (and the miles of orange barrels) slow us down for a half an hour. Settlers traveling west could be delayed for days or even weeks if they had to travel farther up or down the river to find a suitable fording spot.

Purpose:

To allow students to first plan a simple westward route between two points, to estimate travel time, and then contrast it to the estimated travel time a pioneer might face.

Procedure:

1. For this activity students will need a road map of a state or set of states or of the United States. Begin by having students choose two points or cities on the map, one being west of the other. The easternmost point represents the starting place; the westernmost point represents the destination.

2. Have students plan routes using the highway system. Using the scale of miles or the mileage amounts shown on the map, have them determine the total miles for the trip.

3. Using 55 miles per hour for highways and 35 miles per hour for city roads as a guide, have students calculate the amount of time it would take them today to get from starting point to destination.

4. Finally, have students recalculate the same route for the pioneer. Use one and a half or two miles per hour as the rate of travel.

5. Have students adjust the pioneer travel time to take into account natural hazards that appear on the map. For example, if the road crosses a river they must allow an extra half day. If it is a big river, allow a full day. If the highway passes through mountains, students will need to double the travel time for that portion of the trip.

6. Give students time to report their results to the rest of the class. Then have them discuss how the extra time would complicate the trip and how they would make allowances for these complications.

7. As a follow-up have students investigate the same trip's travel time by air. Have them call an airline and find out where the nearest airports are and the amount of time for that trip. If car travel would be necessary between airport and destination, have students further calculate and add that time.

8. This activity can even be set up as a center with predetermined starting spots and destinations for which students must calculate the two travel times.

The Wagon

Some of the first wagons were not much more than pushcarts that the pioneers dragged with them as they walked westward through the Appalachian foothills. As roads improved, wagons drawn by two to four mules or oxen became more practical for not only the traveler but mostly for the freight handler.

The most famous of these first wagons was the Conestoga wagon. These sturdy and durable wagons were made by the Pennsylvania Germans. They were designed specifically for hauling freight and families across the miles of crude roads throughout the Old West. They were built with high wheels so that the axles could easily clear tree stumps left in the road, stumps that could be 15 inches high.

The bed of this wagon was bowed downward in the middle and had high raking ends. This allowed the load to settle into the middle even when steep hills were being negotiated. Heavy canvas was stretched over hoops that were attached to each side. On the back of the wagon a trough was attached from which the animals ate. The driver had no perch up front from which to drive the team. Instead he usually sat on the horse located on the left side nearest the wagon. This position kept him to the right side of the road and established the custom which we still follow today. An assistant or fellow traveler could sit on a "lazy board" located on the left side.

The tough running gear of the wagon was made of several different woods to accommodate the extremely heavy load it had to carry. Empty weight of this wagon was one and a half tons. Fully loaded the weight could exceed six tons. For the westward traveling pioneer of the Old West the distances were not so great and the roads not so bad that a heavy load was impossible to manage. For the freight haulers, the ability to carry that much weight was a necessity.

The Wagon (continued)

When it came time to move across the prairie and through the mountains, the style of the wagon had to change. The sheer weight of the Conestoga made it impractical. Its empty weight of one and a half tons alone was an inadvisable amount to expect a team of animals to pull for five or six months. In addition, the fording of streams and rivers would be impossible when the weight caused the wagon to sink in the soft ground.

Consequently, the Conestoga had to be adapted. The result was the prairie schooner. The prairie schooner got its name because long rows of these vehicles looked like a fleet of ships moving across the plains.

The running gear (i.e., iron wheels, tongue, and axles) was usually made in a wagon shop by an expert who could put together this most important part of the wagon. The wheels were wider than the Conestoga's so that they would be less likely to sink in mud. The front wheels were four feet in diameter while the back wheels would be five to six feet across. These smaller front wheels allowed the wagon to make sharp turns on narrow trails in the mountains. The first prairie schooners were brakeless, but soon pioneers learned that a way of controlling the wagon on steep downgrades was needed to avoid calamities. It was not unusual for these pioneers to carry an extra axle since a broken axle on the trip was irreparable.

The bed was made by the pioneer himself. It was flat instead of curved like the Conestoga's, and its dimensions were 10 feet long, 4 feet wide, and 2 feet deep. The hoops that supported the canvas were big enough to allow an adult to stand upright while standing in the bed. The canvas itself was often double layered and then covered with linseed oil or paint to waterproof it.

To make river crossing possible, the bed was designed to be removed from the running gear. This way the bed could be made water-tight with some tallow and floated across deep rivers.

ACTIVITY *Adapting Transportation*

To get across the prairies and mountains the Conestoga wagon had to be changed. Its strength and weight, which were assets on the roads of the East, were a liability on the roadless plains. Today we still adapt and design vehicles to serve special purposes. This adaptation is most noticeable in the cars we drive.

Have students work in pairs or small teams of three and develop a comparison of two cars that are obviously designed for different travel situations. The different categories of cars include compact cars, midsize sedans, luxury cars, minivans, station wagons, standard vans, pick-up trucks, and recreational vehicles.

First students will need to decide on the categories of comparison. This may include items such as maneuverability, size, storage space, horsepower, travel distance between fill-ups, and options. They can then create a chart that will allow them to more dramatically see the differences in these categories. Make the chart expandable because as students begin to really analyze the two vehicles they will start to think of categories they did not originally identify.

In analyzing the cars, try to get students to focus on objective information first. Owner's manuals and brochures available through car dealerships can provide facts such as trunk space in cubic feet, horsepower, and mileage. If possible, have students inspect the vehicles firsthand to include their own subjective data. They may find out, for example, that although a minivan advertises more overall space, little of it could be used for transporting luggage or goods because most of the space is designed for seating.

When the analysis is done, students develop conclusions about the suitability of each vehicle for specific transportation conditions. All modern vehicles can be used in a variety of situations. The focus here is to get students to decide for what situations a particular vehicle is best suited. An RV can be driven in the city, but it is hardly suited for this type of driving. It is possible to drive a compact car cross-country, but other vehicles will handle the mountains better.

Allow students to present their findings to the class in an oral presentation or in the form of a chart/diagram that they design and display. This activity, once begun, requires little to no additional class time.

When they are done, students may be better able to understand how the design of the wagon was crucial to the success the pioneers had in crossing the prairie.

The Squeaky Wheel

The most important part of the prairie schooner was the axle, and the most critical part of the axle was the hub. The hub was the end of the axle where the wheel was attached. The constant spinning motion of the hub as the wheel turned meant that the greatest amount of friction was experienced at this point. On a 2,000-mile trip it was not long before an all-too-familiar squeak developed on any or all of the four wheels.

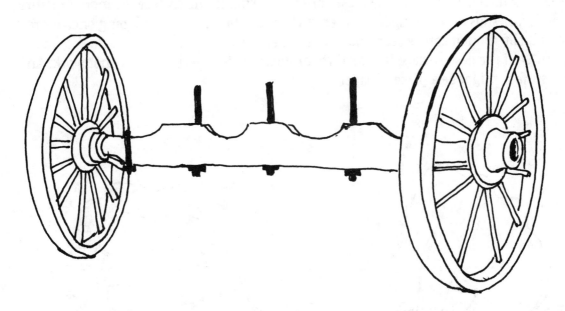

The squeak was not the problem, but it was a sign of a much bigger problem, friction. Friction caused a wearing away of the hub and would eventually cause the axle to break down. To remedy this problem the traveling settler carried a bucket of lubricant that dangled from a peg in the axle. This lubricant was made of animal fat mixed with tar. The animal fat was the lubricant while the tar helped to keep the lubricant on the hub once it was applied.

The squeaky wheel of the prairie schooner provides an interesting science connection with the study of lubricants, but first students need to know what a squeak is.

ACTIVITY *What Is a Squeak?*

The best way to describe a squeak is that it is a series of very fast stick-and-slip movements. Students will better understand this if they perform a simple experiment. Have students place their erasers on their desks at a 45° angle (see diagram 1). Instruct each to apply a small amount of pressure downward and to push the pencil forward slowly. At first the eraser may slide across the desk surface. Next, tell students to press down harder and push forward faster. This will cause greater friction which will result in the eraser briefly sticking to the surface. As more pressure is applied, the eraser slips forward suddenly, then sticks again briefly before slipping once more. This stick-and-slip motion can be seen and felt as the eraser moves across the surface of the desk (see diagram 2). If the desk surface is at all dirty or greasy, this experiment may not work. An alternative surface might be a piece of paper.

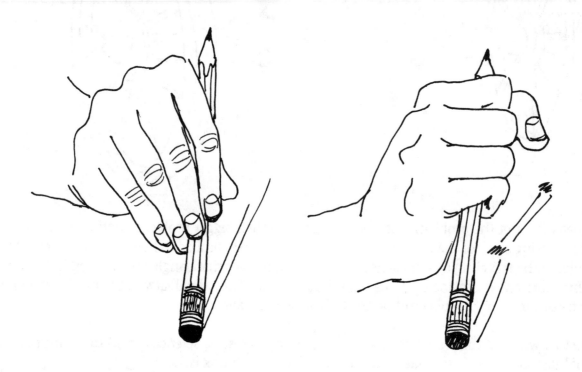

DEMONSTRATION *Creating a Squeak*

You may want to ask students why they cannot hear a squeaky sound with this experiment. It is because the two surfaces, rubber and plastic, do not create that sound. You can demonstrate a squeaky sound for students by using a glass (preferably a wine or water glass with a stem). Lightly wet your finger and begin rubbing around the edge of the glass. As friction begins to develop, a sound will become audible. If you use a crystal glass, a resonation will develop that creates a high-pitched tone.

Students can apply what they have learned by locating places at home where squeaks can occur. Any place where two metal surfaces create friction needs to be lubricated, or a squeak will occur. Have students go home and list all the places in their houses where they know two metal surfaces could rub together creating a squeaking sound. Hinges are the most obvious, but they may realize that parts of machines, such as washers and dryers, are potential squeakers as well as bedsprings, electric can openers, garage doors, and just about anything found in a car.

Metal, of course, is not the only material that can make a squeak. Wood can squeak as well. Students are certain to have squeaky steps and floors. The principle, however, is always the same. Friction causes a stick-and-slip movement that makes a squeak if it happens quickly enough.

ACTIVITY *Lubricants*

The formula for stopping a squeak is fairly simple. Reduce the friction and the stick-and-slip motion will stop. No more squeak.

The pioneers solved the friction problem with a lubricant made mostly of animal fat. As it turns out, this was an excellent choice. Animal fats are semisolid lubricants and resist being squeezed out. Thus, under the heavy load of the wagon bed the lubricant that the pioneer applied was most useful.

You can easily get students to understand this idea of lubricants and their roles in reducing friction. Once students have successfully created the slip-and-stick condition with the pencil eraser, have them apply a small amount of water to the surface of the desk. Then have them try the same experiment. No matter how much more pressure they apply, the eraser will slip on the wet surface. Why? Because the water acts as a lubricant and reduces the friction between the eraser and the surface of the desk.

Not Just for Wheels

As civilization progressed farther west, it brought with it all the civilized contraptions of the East. From small mechanical apple peelers to water pumps used on farms to huge machinery used in the silver mines of Nevada, lubricants were needed to prevent metal parts from wearing out or breaking. Animal fat was not the perfect remedy. Eventually mineral lubricants were discovered, leading to a huge business that still exists today.

ACTIVITY   *Testing Lubricants*

Anything that reduces friction between two surfaces is a lubricant. As the students saw, water can be a lubricant. Unfortunately, water does not make a very good lubricant because it dries quickly and can easily be squeezed out from between the two surfaces it is lubricating. Thicker liquids can lubricate better.

Students can test the lubrication ability of different liquids and solids if you are willing to prepare for a small mess. Begin by bringing some household materials that act like lubricants (you may be able to have students contribute some of these things). These might include dish soap, vegetable oil, furniture wax, baby powder, or whatever students can think of that has a lubricating property.

Put students into lab groups of two to four and tell each group to bring several small shallow dishes or margarine container tops and several pennies. You will also need to provide paper towels and access to some water.

Students are to put a penny on the dish and pick it up. Have them note how easy this is. Now add one of the lubricants to the dish (e.g., pour some dish soap on the penny) and have them try to pick it up again. The fact that there is less friction between the finger and penny will make it more difficult.

Students can repeat this with all the lubricants they brought and then rate them when they are finished. Discuss the use of dry lubricants vs. liquid lubricants. Dry lubricants do not squeeze out from between two surfaces as easily as wet ones. Graphite in pencils is an example of a dry lubricant also used in plumbing.

CHAPTER FIVE
Shelter for the Pioneer

It Depended on Where They Were

Few aspects of frontier life were more dependent on location than that of shelter. In the eighteenth century settlers coming from the East to the Piedmont Region were used to clapboard-style houses. If they came from money they might be more used to brick or stone homes. Both styles took more time, effort, and skill than a solitary pioneer or even a pioneer family had when they arrived at their destination. Getting something over their heads was urgent business, so they needed to use what was provided by their natural setting.

Seventy years later when the pioneers came from east of the Mississippi to the plains, they knew best how to build homes made only of wood. The prairie, however, did not offer timber. These pioneers had to develop their own style of home until wood could be brought in. These circumstances resulted in sod homes.

In the Southwest, nature offered little of either wood or sod. Here, adobe bricks became the building material of choice. Most of the early settlers of this region arrived from their homelands with knowledge of adobe brick.

What is important for students to realize is that the resourcefulness of the pioneers was needed if they were to adapt to the new surroundings that their location offered.

The Log Cabin

The log cabin is often erroneously associated with the English colonists who first arrived in America. To be certain, the log cabin was used during colonial times but not by the English colonists on the eastern seaboard. Instead, it was the Swedish and Finnish colonists of the late 1600s who first brought this style of house to America. The settlers who moved farther inland toward the Piedmont and then across the Appalachians were the ones who made it most popular.

The log cabin was a natural building style for the woodland areas of the Eastern Mississippi Region. The settlers who moved into this area mistakenly believed that fertile farm soil lay beneath all the decaying leaf humus. The fact was that the most fertile soil was to be found in the plains areas. Nonetheless, thousands of pioneer families cleared the woodland areas to get at what they believed was the same rich soil in which huge oaks, pines, firs, and maples grew. The logs from these trees became the walls and flooring of the easily recognized log cabin.

One major attraction of the log cabin was the relative ease with which it could be built. With little more than ax and an oxen team, it was possible for a single person to build a log cabin. Granted, it was a lot more difficult under these conditions and the final product was undoubtedly quite rustic, but it was possible. Such an operation would take weeks, so until such a cabin could be built a lean-to was used for housing the family. The lean-to was in many ways a quick and temporary version of the log cabin. It was called a half-faced camp and could be erected in a single day.

A pair of forked poles were positioned about 10 feet apart. Across the top a pole was placed in the forks. Smaller logs were leaned against one side to create a roof and back. More logs were stacked horizontally to make the sides. Bark would cover the roof and sides to keep out the rain. The front was left open; this was where a fire was made.

 FS-10140 Life as a Pioneer

Make no mistake, building any substantial housing is a formidable task. The clapboard style imported by the English colonists, however, required more skill and artistry than the average person had. In fact, skilled craftsmen were imported to New England to help with the design, layout, and construction of these homes. Such luxury was impossible to the westward-moving pioneer.

As mentioned above, a log cabin could be built by a single person with little more than an ax. This was seldom the case. As settlers moved into an area they naturally banded together into communities. Helping a newcomer erect a log cabin home was a favor no one would turn down. With several families helping, the entire process could be completed in a matter of days.

A great deal of ingenuity has gone into the development of the log cabin, which is still being used today in many locations around the United States. Below are some of the design problems that pioneers faced. Use this list to stimulate class discussion or as a resource if you choose to do the activity entitled "How to Build a Log Cabin."

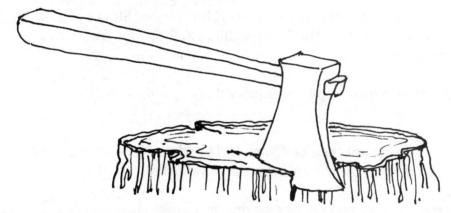

1. The four logs that form the base of the cabin began rotting if they touched the ground. This weakened the structure so that within five to ten years it had to be rebuilt.

2. Pioneers had to develop a way of raising the logs, which were stacked horizontally, to the height of about seven feet to create the first floor, even higher for the loft.

3. Nails were an item of luxury for the first pioneers and for many of the settlers that followed. Therefore, they had to create a way to hold the cedar shingles in place on their slanted roof.

4. Stone chimneys for fireplaces take lots of time and effort. Another style of chimney had to be designed that could be put up within a day's time.

5. Door and window openings required too much skill to be built in as the walls were going up.

6. Round logs are terribly irregular. Wind and cold air would blow through the openings between them.

7. Moss began growing on the roof within a year's time.

8. Metal door hinges simply did not exist for the pioneer.

9. Every door needed a locking system.

10. The notched corner construction of the log cabin prevents lengthening the walls of the cabin if a pioneer later wants to add on to the original construction.

Anyone looking at a picture of a log cabin can easily see the simple design of the building. Most people do not realize the engineering difficulties involved in erecting just the walls of the log cabin, let alone the roof. The following activity will give students the opportunity to play the role of a log cabin engineer.

Purpose:
To develop an awareness of the practical problems pioneers faced in designing and building a log cabin.

Procedure:
1. Place students in small groups of about three or four. Tell each group that they are a team of engineers whose job it is to write out the steps to making a log cabin.

2. Hand out copies of the student activity page entitled "How to Build a Log Cabin." It also would be handy to have some pictures of log cabins available for students to look at as they plan their procedure.

3. Have students develop their step-by-step procedures according to the activity sheet's guidelines.

4. Allow each group to present their design plan to the class. Make notes during each presentation of problems the students may have overlooked.

Most of the plans that students make will be lacking details. Becoming aware of these details is the focus of the next step.

5. Begin to ask probing questions about their design plan. The list on the previous page is a good start. As students begin to focus on the actual details involved in building a log cabin they will add to the list.

6. Create a list of design problems and allow different teams of engineers the job of solving them. You may want to allow students a few days to work on some of these problems so that they can use outside resources to arrive at an answer.

7. Have student teams report on how they solved the problem. The page following the activity discusses the actual method used by pioneers in erecting a log cabin in the first half century of the 1800s (before nails).

How to Build a Log Cabin

The process of building a log cabin was developed and refined over many years. It was one of the easiest of shelters to build but still presented problems to the builder. Acting as a team of engineers, develop a step-by-step process for building a log cabin. The format below will guide you in developing those steps.

Step One—Visualize

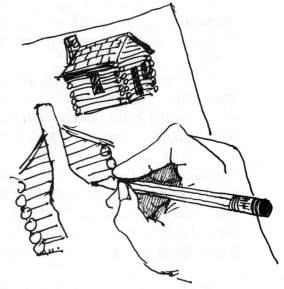

Engineers often begin a project by first developing a picture or model of the final product. It would help if you had a picture of a log cabin so that you could better see what the final product would look like. If that is not possible, take time to sketch a few pictures of what you imagine the log cabin will look like when completed. It is a good idea to sketch the cabin from several different angles (front, side, etc.). As you progress through the steps, use this sketching technique to help you visualize any step that is hard to put into words.

Step Two—The Main Parts

Since all parts of a log cabin are not erected at the same time, a general plan of action needs to be developed. Begin by making a list of the main steps involved in making the cabin (for example, gathering logs, building the chimney).

When that list is done, organize the steps in the order in which they would be done.

Step Three—Add the Details

Now go back and for each major step add the details which explain how that step is to be accomplished. As you work on this step your team may realize that some main steps are missing or that the steps are in the wrong order. If so, just go back and make changes.

Step Four—Analyze

By the time you are done your team may realize that certain steps are not planned perfectly. Since none of you have probably ever built a log cabin before, that is to be expected. Go back now and evaluate each step. Make a list of problems you see with your plan that might need to be worked out before it could be put into action.

How a Log Cabin Was Actually Built

Below is a summary of how a log cabin might have been built in the early nineteenth century. The numbers in parentheses correspond to the problems posed on page 53.

The first job in making a log cabin was to secure the logs. A single pioneer might take the time to cut down the 80 or more logs before inviting his neighbors to a log raisin'. Everyone who came planned to stay for about four days and may have brought their own food with the host supplying the liquid refreshment.

When everyone had assembled, the logs were hauled to the building site with oxen or mules. There they were further cut to the proper length and notched. Today's modern log cabins are built to look rustic, so the roundness of the log is kept. The pioneer, however, was more concerned about a tight seal between logs. Consequently, most cabins were made of logs that were squared. (6) This was more time consuming, but resulted in a notch that fit more tightly and fewer spaces between logs as they were stacked horizontally. Squaring logs was accomplished by laying out a chalk line as a guide on each side of the log. The axman then scored the log to this line. These sections are then easily split off with a broad ax, producing a flat side (see illustration A). Finally, the end notches are carved that will hold the logs in place and allow the length of each log to lay flush with the others.

In laying the first logs the pioneer wanted to keep them off the ground. Several large, flat stones were placed at each corner and the bottom logs were placed on them. (1) This design required a floor for the log house instead of the dirt floor of many early models. To accomplish this the bottom logs of two parallel sides were notched and floor joists were laid down. Floor boards could then be laid on top of these joists (see illustration B).

Stacking the logs was easy at first, especially if two or more pioneers were available to lift. Anything beyond waist height, however, required that the builders roll the logs up to the next level (see illustration C). Two logs on the ends were rolled and then two on the sides. Each time the logs were placed in the end notches. At the seven-foot level, the first stage of the cabin was built. (2)

With the first floor of the cabin finished, the builders could more easily split into teams. One team could start cutting out the door and window frames as well as the fireplace. This was done with the use of an auger to make the initial holes. A pointed saw was then used to make the rough cut that would become the window or door. (5) Around this rough cut a frame was installed made of planks hewn from logs. The planks were fitted into the doorway; an auger would make a hole in both the plank and the log end behind it, and a wooden peg was hammered into it to secure the frame to the opening (see illustration D). Window frames were made the same way.

How a Log Cabin Was Actually Built (continued)

Hinges for doors and window shutters were handled a number of different ways. Leather acted as a supple hinge in a pinch. Placing two pegs so that they stuck out of the top and bottom of the door allowed them to act as hinges when placed in holes augered into the frame (see illustration E). (8)

The matter of a fireplace and chimney was handled a little differently. After the opening for the fireplace had been cut out and lined with stone, a catted chimney was built. This was a structure running along the outside of the house made of smaller logs notched and stacked in the same manner as the frame of the home. The inside of this structure was thickly coated with mud to protect it against the heat of the fire. (4) When the pioneer had time later, he could replace the catted chimney with fireproof stone (see illustration F).

As the doors, windows, and fireplace were being built, a roof could also be laid. With the first story finished, about eight or nine notches could be put into the top logs, the same as the bottom logs had. Into these notches joists were laid for the loft. Floorboards could be laid across these joists. To complete the roof it was necessary to make a slanted gable at each end of the cabin. A ridgepole was placed atop the last log connecting the two gables at the top. From this ridgepole a lattice of rafters and room beams was created. It was to this lattice work that the shingles were attached. The shingle was attached and kept in place by weight logs tied to the roof beams thus clamping the shingles down (see illustration G). (3)

A shingle was usually made of cedar-type wood that split straight. The splitting was done with special tools called a froe and a maul (see illustration H). Although moss would quickly grow on the roof, the pioneer did not mind. The moss allowed the shingle to swell quickly in a rainstorm closing each crack or hole and making for a drier inside. (7)

Sealing the house was an important step in finishing the job. Mud or clay was brought up from a nearby creek or pond. It was spread along each seam between logs. (6) This process, called chinking, was not a one-time effort. Chinking was often done on a yearly basis because the mud or clay would wear away with the weather. To help keep the mud or clay as firm as possible, sticks, stones, and grass were sometimes mixed in with it.

The log house was sufficient for the young pioneer family. As the family grew, however, an addition may have become necessary. The notched corners of the cabin prevented the type of additions used by the eastern colonists. Instead a completely new cabin was built a few feet from the old cabin and the two were connected with a common roof. Only a breezeway separated them. (10)

Illustrations for How a Log Cabin Was Actually Built

First Homes on the Prairie

The pioneers that settled the plains had the advantage of time. Whereas the pioneers of the Eastern and Western Mississippi Frontiers settled in the first half of the nineteenth century, settlers in the plains area of Kansas, Oklahoma, Nebraska, the Dakotas, as well as eastern Colorado, Wyoming, and Montana did not get going until after the Civil War. This was no coincidence. The lack of timber, thick grass, and dry conditions made farming impractical given the technology that existed in the first half of the 1800s. Furthermore, the prairie lacked the promise of mineral wealth that attracted settlers to the Pacific Frontier.

Advances in technology finally made settlement of the plains possible. Consequently, when pioneers began moving into this area they had the advantage of railways for goods and personal transportation, as well as improved farming equipment. This, however, is where the advantage of the plains pioneer ends, for the biggest obstacle to living on the prairie could be overcome only by grit and ingenuity. That obstacle was having no wood for building a shelter.

Like all his pioneer predecessors, the plains settler arrived at his plot of land with the barest of necessities that would enable him or her to survive. The first order of business was to devise a temporary shelter that would last until a more permanent one could be built. Tents might be used at first, but the howling prairie winds quickly made these impractical. A more likely solution became the dugout. The dugout was cousin to the half-faced camp of the woodland pioneer. A settler simply dug out the side of a hill or rise. He supported it with wood, if he could find some or if he had brought any, and built a fire in front of it. Some dugouts were elaborate in comparison to others. An early Nebraska settler included a door and windows in his, while others dug a hole in the roof right through the top of the rise and installed a fireplace.

Once in the dugout, pioneers easily recognized advantages to this crude form of shelter. These shelters were cool in the summer and warm in the winter. They did an excellent job of protecting the pioneer family from incessant wind and occasional brushfires. Unfortunately, these dugouts were also dark, damp, and buggy . . . excellent conditioning for the eventual improved version that most prairie pioneers would call their home, the sod house.

59   FS-10140 Life as a Pioneer

Soddies

Sod is defined as a section of grass-covered topsoil held together by matted roots. On the prairie the only thing there was plenty of was sod. Therefore, it was the most natural building material for the pioneer to use.

Improvements in the plow were one of the innovations that allowed the pioneer to make his sod home. As early as 1838 John Deere and Leonard Andrus had designed a plow with a steel share (cutting edge) that kept the sod from sticking to the share as it tore through the ground. Subsequent improvements led to a plow that would cut the sod while still keeping the dirt and roots intact. As these prairie farmers cut through the sod they naturally earned the name "sodbusters."

About an acre and a half of sod was needed to make a sod house, also called a *soddie*. Bricks of the sod were dug out and hauled to the home site by wagon. The bricks were always laid the same day they were cut to hold in the moisture and keep them firm. Each block of sod was about three feet long, one and a half feet wide, and four inches thick.

The making of a sod house did not require as much engineering ability as did a log house. Where the log house builder had to pay particular attention to hewing and notching logs to make them as airtight as possible, the soddie builder was working with a very forgiving material. The sod bricks he dug up, also called "Nebraska marble," fit tightly together in a double-thick wall (see illustration below). Spaces between bricks were filled with mud or dirt, but the nature of the sod did not require the kind of yearly attention that was involved in chinking the log home.

If a sodbuster were lucky enough to have land through which a river flowed, he might find a patch of cottonwood trees. These would supply the wood he needed for a door, roof frame, and window frame. If not, he had to have some lumber shipped by rail to a nearby town where he would go to pick it up with his wagon. Two forked poles held up a ridgepole. From this ridgepole the roof frame was built. First grasses, then sod were layed on this slanted frame to make an airtight (but not watertight) roof. Often a large muslin sheet was draped below the frame inside the soddie to catch falling debris.

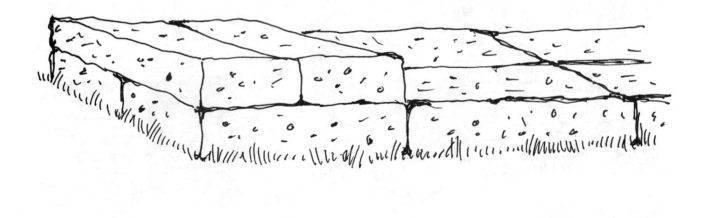

Doors and windows were installed as the walls went up. Wooden frames were used to support the weight of the sod walls. Although glass windows were certainly not part of the early sodbuster's home, contact with ever-growing towns and railway systems made it possible for many later soddies to include these luxuries.

Soddies lasted only about 10 years before rain and the elements made them unlivable. As soon as a prairie pioneer could afford it, he had plank lumber shipped in for the building of a proper home. Additions, on the other hand, were much easier than with a log house since walls could be easily taken down or extended.

These sod homes were dark, damp, and generally about as inconvenient as living in a dirt hole. The sodbuster had mice, insects, and snakes literally drop in from the roof at any time. Canopied beds may have looked out of place in such a rustic setting but they certainly provided a safer night's sleep. There are even recorded instances of a wayward cow coming through the roof of a sod house that had been built into the side of a hill. Some women had their children hold an umbrella over the food as it cooked on the iron stove during a morning rain. Living in such a domicile created dirt, and by today's standards everyone who lived in a soddie looked like he or she needed a bath.

Many pioneer families went to great lengths to make such a place homey. Interior walls sometimes were wallpapered or covered with canvas. Rugs were laid down (or anything to keep the dust from being kicked up). From the East a family might bring furniture such as a wardrobe, tables, chairs, and beds. Some pioneer families even brought sewing machines and organs. A cast iron stove was a necessity.

What was the cost of this type of home? Unbelievably inexpensive. The sod was free, and so was the backache. Stovepipe, nails, door latch, lumber, and a window might cost only about three dollars. For the just-starting plains pioneer, it was a real deal.

ACTIVITY   *What Is in a Brick of Nebraska Marble?*

The sod that the prairie pioneer used for his home was already the home of countless life forms. When a brick of Nebraska marble was dug up and made into a part of a wall, all the creatures living in that brick became the sodbuster's instant roommates. Having students closely inspect a piece of sod will reveal this.

Purpose:

Students will examine and record the composition and life forms found in a small brick of sod.

Procedure:

1. Divide students into lab teams of about four and hand out the lab guideline sheets found on pages 63 and 64.

2. Obtain a small brick of sod for each team. The brick should be at least six inches long, three inches wide and four inches thick. The four-inch depth is important. It would be great if each team could have a standard 3' x 1½ foot piece but that could lead to a lot of barren ground.

   The sod should be natural, certainly not purchased from a landscaper. The landscape sod is without all the creatures found in nature.

   You may even want to dig up a standard sod brick and divide it among the teams to represent what a sodbuster would have used.

   Take students along on the dig and allow them to select the site(s) from which it comes. A variety of sites can make for interesting comparisons.

3. Have students record from where the sod was taken and return to the classroom. If the sod pieces are not going to be used for awhile, preserve them in plastic bags to retain the moisture.

4. Allow teams to examine and record their piece of "Nebraska marble." Emphasize the need to work methodically and to record everything carefully. If possible, provide magnifying glasses or hand-held microscopes for closer inspection.

5. Students should save all pieces and return them to the original site when finished.

6. Discuss student observations, noting differences if sites differed. Depth of roots, difference in soil composition, compactness of soil, presence of stones, presence of insect eggs or larvae, different plant and animal life should all be noted.

7. A chart or diagram of student findings can be created and made into a bulletin board.

8. The student activity sheet is set up to have students create a notebook of their observations. This can become a form of assessment. Encourage complete sentence observations. Part four can be used as part of the notebook or as the discussion question when students are finished.

What Is in a Brick of Nebraska Marble?

The sodbusters of the plains states brought a lot more into their homes than just dirt when they built their soddies. Among the dirt and roots were many other things. The purpose of this lab is to discover the abundance of living and nonliving matter found in a section of sod.

Working as a team, use a small notebook to record what you observed when examining a small brick of sod.

Part One—Location

1. Record from where your sod section was taken.

2. Record the time of year.

3. If possible, draw a small map showing where the sod was taken in relation to other land features nearby, such as hills and trees.

4. Record the dimensions of the sod piece.

Part Two—A Quick Examination (no poking or prying necessary)

1. Record the type of plant life that is living on the top of the sod piece.

2. Record what kind of living or nonliving matter is found at the base of the grass (lying on top of the soil).

3. Record the depth of the roots of the grass growing in the sod. You will need to decide on the average depth.

4. Record any change in color of the soil that occurs in the four inches of depth. Record at what depth level these changes occur.

5. Record observable stones, twigs, worm holes, etc. that can be seen without taking the sod piece apart.

6. Draw a diagram of this sod piece showing the above items.

Part Three—A Close Examination

1. Take hold of some grass between your finger and thumb and try to pull it out. Note if it tore off or pulled out roots and all.

2. Begin at the bottom and begin shaving off dirt. Record everything you come across and at what level it is. Work your way up toward the surface.

3. If you have a magnifying glass or a hand-held microscope, carefully inspect different layers of the sod. Record what you see. Look for insect eggs and larva as well as small insects and plants.

4. Diagram those things not already shown in the diagram from part three.

Part Four—Conclusions

Write a paragraph in which you discuss what the pioneer family would bring into the house by using such a piece of sod. Include both living and nonliving items. If eggs and larva were found, speculate as to when they might hatch. How would that affect life in the home? What would the home smell like, look like, and feel like, based on your observation of sod?

Now evaluate whether you think your piece would make good wall material. Take into account the following questions: Was the depth of the roots sufficient to hold the piece together? Was the type of soil solid enough to hold together in a rain storm? Were other materials in the soil likely to hold it together?

Tie-in Information About Grasses and Grassland

Below are some interesting points you may want to include as students discuss their findings following the sod examination lab.

1. Many explorers before the sodbusters found the grasslands a place unfit for survival. Coronado in the sixteenth century found the country totally unsuitable for habitation. Both the Lewis and Clark expedition and the Pike expedition spoke and wrote unfavorably of the dry grasslands which they likened to a desert.

2. The grasslands found in the middle of our country are really two distinct grassland areas. The first extends from the Mississippi River to about the ninety-eighth meridian. These grasses are tall (the native grasses were up to eight feet tall) and are provided with plenty of water as warm moist air from the Gulf of Mexico brings abundant rain (20 inches per year).

3. The drier grassland area from the ninety-eighth meridian to the Rocky Mountains receives as little as five inches of rainfall a year. Winds moving over the Rockies release their moisture on the western side of the mountains, leaving dry air to blow across this expanse of grassland. The grasses here grow smaller (a native grass called buffalo grass grows about 20 inches tall) but are heartier.

4. The grassland area is very fertile compared to the woodland areas east of the Mississippi River. Geologically this is due to the upheaval of the Rocky Mountains 60 million years ago and then again 15 million years ago. As rains washed away mineral-rich silt, it was gradually deposited in a band sloping toward the Mississippi River. Hundreds of thousands of years ago glaciers left a deposit of rich silt that winds blew south into the grassland area. Finally, each year as grassland fires destroy the tops of the plants, they provide nutrients for the soil. The strong roots of these grasses erupt into life again in the spring.

5. The roots of the grasses found in the prairie may provide an extreme contrast to the roots that your students observed. Despite ample rainfall, few trees grow west of the Mississippi River. What is keeping them from growing? The answer is the grasses. The extensive root system of these grasses interweave to create an impenetrable wall at the top of the soil. One rye grass plant grown experimentally put out a total of 378 miles of roots in four months. No seed from a tree could possibly compete with that for water and soil. Pioneers digging up sod had a formidable opponent. No wonder the biggest problem was often broken plow shares.

The sodbuster brought even more than creatures into his sod home. Billions of microscopic animals and plants made the surface area of the sod their home, too.

The microscopic world is the focus of this activity. It does require access to a microscope, slide, and cover slip. This activity is equally possible to do if you are focusing on a woodland environment. Instead of obtaining grasses, try using some decaying leaves.

Purpose:

To acquaint students with the existence of microscopic life that is around them.

Procedure:

1. Obtain a large handful of grass from a nearby field or vacant lot. Include in your handful some of the decaying grass and plant life found just at the surface level. Also dig slightly below the surface and get a small amount of dirt.

   If you did the sod lab described earlier, just get some of these "fixin's" from one of the lab teams before they return it.

2. Place the material in a bowl and cover it with water from the tap. Then cover that with a piece of aluminum foil and let it set in a warm place for a few days. Avoid disturbing it.

3. Have students prepare a piece of paper by drawing a circle on it. This circle represents the circular view through the microscope's lens.

4. After the few days, remove the foil. If you notice a smell when the foil is removed you will know everything is working just fine. Lightly stir the water. With an eyedropper have students take a sample from near some of the plant material and prepare a slide.

5. Have students view the slide and record what they see by drawing it on the prepared paper. If no creatures are seen, have students take different samples from different areas of the water or even wait a little longer. In time, students will be able to actually see different types of microscopic life at different depth levels.

6. Discuss with students whether this type of life may have had an impact on the life of the pioneers who brought it with them as part of their homes.

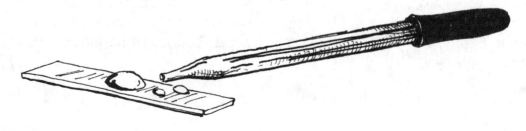

CHAPTER SIX
Hunting for Food

Game for the Pioneers

Letters were written home by the pioneers telling of the abundance of game and wild foods growing in the frontier. The promise of such an easy way of life certainly lured many more settlers westward. These accounts were accurate only part of the time. Today, we like to imagine that a walk in the forest during the early 1800s would result in the spotting of hundreds of animals. That was not the case. Although hunting was definitely the means for survival for early pioneers, it was not as easy as a walk in the woods. With the right skill and tools it could be easy, but few first-time settlers had those skills. They had to learn the hard way (through trial and error) or by having someone else show them the ropes.

Arrival at the frontier homestead and the building of shelter rarely left time for planting and harvesting. First-year pioneers almost always relied on hunting and trapping for the supply of food that first year. Even after the first year, catching game was a necessary part of daily pioneer life. Only after years of living on and improving their land might a pioneer family be able to grow enough of its own grain, vegetables, and livestock to no longer rely on hunting and trapping.

The Game

Big game included moose, deer, elk, buffalo, and bear, depending on the frontier location. A single deer could provide enough venison for a week or more. Large game, however, was not always available. Annual migration patterns could leave the settlers with no large game within a day's walking distance. During these times the pioneer turned to the smaller game that remained in one environment all year. Rabbits, beavers, raccoons, squirrels, opossum, and even skunks, as well as turkey, prairie dog, quail, and any fish found in a nearby lake or river, all made edible fare. Shooting these animals was possible but tricky. It took a good shot to hit a small and elusive creature. Trapping was a more likely method.

Pioneer traps were as varied as can be imagined. The most desirable trap was the steel spring trap used as early as the eighteenth century in the Maine frontier. They firmly secured the animal until the settler arrived. The early pioneers may not have had such a luxury. Snares made of rope that caught the animal around the neck were common. Pitfalls, log pens, or even devices that brought a rock or log crashing down on the animal's head were also used.

For most pioneers, however, the rifle was the most important instrument for catching game. The musket that sprayed birdshot was ineffective at bringing down medium to large game. A single-shot rifle was needed and that meant only one shot to kill or sufficiently wound an animal. Most pioneers became excellent marksmen. Nonetheless, skill in stalking the animals was needed to get close enough for a sure shot.

Some Basic Trap Designs

1. Pitfalls—These were pits dug deep enough to entrap a large animal. After the pit was dug the opening was disguised and baited. One design had a trap door mounted on a center post. As the animal walked onto the door it would swing down under its weight and the animal would fall in the pit. Another way of disguising the openings was with very light branches covered with leaves that would collapse under a large animal's weight.

2. Snares—Rope or twine was placed in a spot through which the animal frequently passed. After the head of the animal made it through the loop, forward movement tightened the knot around its neck. When attached to a bent sapling the struggling animal would trigger it and snap its neck. Another method had the rope tied to the middle of a long branch. When the animal became snared it would run into the brush where the branch would snag, thus securing the animal until the hunter came back.

3. Log pens—Similar to pitfalls, a log cage was made and baited. When the animal entered, it triggered the door to close and trapped the animal. Such a cage was also made for turkeys. A trail of corn led to the pen and under a hole dug beneath one of the sides. The turkey entered the pen eating the corn. When it raised its head, it no longer saw the hole and was trapped.

4. Catching birds—Birds were especially elusive to the pioneer hunter. They frightened easily, roosted high above the ground making traps nearly impossible, and flew high above making shooting most difficult. Pigeons, which were most plentiful in the early 1800s, were caught using nets. First the birds were fed regularly in one area on the ground where a net had been erected. Once the birds grew accustomed to the routine feeding, the net could be dropped and dozens of birds caught. Still another method was to set fires below their roosting trees. In confusion they would swoop down and often become roasted in the process. Dozens could be simply picked up afterward.

The Rifle

The early pioneer's reputation with a rifle is legendary. The Kentucky rifle was probably the first American rifle to gain notoriety. It was originally crafted in Pennsylvania and was known to some as the Pennsylvania rifle. It was about five feet long with an octagonal barrel and a wooden stock that extended the full length of the barrel. The stock was made of a hard wood, usually maple. Beneath the stock was the ramrod, and in the butt end of the stock leather patches and grease were stored.

To load such a gun took about one minute. Gunpowder was placed down the muzzle of the gun. A bullet was then put into a greased leather patch and ramrodded down atop the powder charge. A small bit of powder was placed on the lock and the pan cover was closed. When the lock was cocked the pioneer was ready to fire.

At the beginning of the nineteenth century such a gun was considered a reliable necessity. As the century progressed, guns became more accurate, and the ammunition became self-priming so that by the late 1800s the repeating rifle was the gun of choice for the pioneer.

Stalking Game

Learning the habits of the game was the most important part of becoming a successful hunter. Nature had endowed the game with instincts and senses that the pioneer lacked. A deer, for example, could hear a hunter snap a twig a quarter mile away. At the same distance a bear could smell the pioneer. To overcome these obvious advantages, settlers had to devise ways of either luring the animal closer or find a way of sneaking up on it undetected.

From the wingbone of a turkey some pioneers fashioned an instrument that made the sound of a turkey hen when a man blew into it. Curious gobblers came down from their roosts at such a sound and walked toward it.

Some hunting was done at night to accommodate the nocturnal tendencies of some animals. With a torch in the front of a canoe, a hunter would float downstream. A deer coming to the river to drink would stop and stare at the light, thus enabling the hunter to get off a good shot.

Pioneers quickly became aware of the term "upwind." Human scent is particularly strong to animals and the scent is carried by the wind to their sensitive noses. A hunter would hide in the brush and wait for a deer or elk to follow its normal path to its feeding place at dawn or dusk. By remaining upwind, the animal would be unable to pick up the scent of the hunter allowing for a close shot.

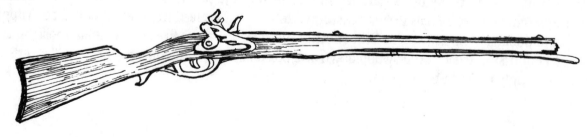

ACTIVITY   *Catching Dinner*

Knowing the habits of the animal was the pioneer's biggest advantage. It led him to the proper location, allowed him to hide undetected, or helped him design a trap that would work. Pioneers gained this knowledge through firsthand experience or learned it from someone else.

Purpose:

Students will devise a way of catching a specific animal after studying the habits of the animal.

Procedure:

1. Decide whether students will work alone or in pairs.

2. Introduce the activity with information about the kinds of animals that pioneers trapped and some of the traps they fashioned.

3. Either assign an animal or allow students to select the type of animal that they would like to study. Below is a list of possibilities.

4. Students will need to decide whether they will be designing a trap for the animal or planning a way of stalking it.

5. Reproduce and hand out the the design guides entitled "Catching Dinner" found on pages 72 and 73.

6. The design guide allows the teacher to decide what kinds of materials students will prepare and present. For example, since students are required to research the animal that they would hunt, a teacher can require a list of sources used as well as notes taken. For assessment, students can be required to either orally or in a paragraph explain what knowledge about the animal led them to the design they developed. Finally, if a teacher wishes, students can have the option of actually building the trap and bringing it in.

7. Allow students to share their trap designs or plans with the class so that they not only show the diagram but also share what they learned about the animal that affected the design.

Animals That Pioneers Trapped or Shot

Bear	Turkey	Beaver	Raccoon	Boar
Wolf	Squirrel	Quail	Porcupine	Geese
Rabbit	Opossum	Prairie Dog	Pigeon	Duck
Bison	Elk	Antelope	Panther	Deer
Moose	Turtle	Sage Goose	Woodchuck	Otter

Catching Dinner

Introduction

The early pioneers did not have the luxury of a town store or restaurant when hunger hit. Dinner often consisted of whatever game could be trapped or shot. A hungry pioneer was either very unlucky or lacked the skill to catch his meal.

Two methods of catching game were available. The preferred method was hunting and shooting. To be successful at this required the skills of stalking and then firing a flintlock rifle. Most animals had senses that prevented a hunter from getting close enough to easily shoot it. Different techniques of stalking the animals allowed the pioneer to do just that. Trapping was the alternative to shooting. A clever trap held an animal in one spot until the hunter returned to kill it.

Both methods required knowledge. To hunt or trap an animal, a pioneer had to know everything he could about that animal. He needed to know its habits, its instincts, its strengths, and its weaknesses. The pioneer needed to know where it made its home, where it ate, and its migration patterns. Without this knowledge, a good shot or a good trap was useless.

Directions

It is your job to design a trap or a plan for stalking an animal that the pioneer would have hunted. You will develop this trap or plan in writing or in a drawing and be ready to present it to the class. To do this you must become knowledgeable in the ways of the animal.

Getting Started

Once you have selected the animal that will be your prey, you will need to research the animal. You can do this by reading as much as you can about the animal. If it is possible to observe the animal (such as with a squirrel), you may also spend time observing and making note of its habits. All this information will be used in developing your plan or trap. On the lines below list information that you know is important in making your plan.

_____

_____

_____

_____

_____

_____

_____

Trapping or Hunting?

After you have done your research, you must decide how the prey will be caught. Small quick animals are probably best trapped since it is nearly impossible to get close enough for a shot at such a quick target. On the other hand large, strong animals require huge, strong traps and may be more easily hunted. Either method is possible with any animal. Your research will give you information that will lead you to this decision.

Which technique will you use? _____

Design It

Once you have decided on the method, you will develop the plan. If your plan is to trap the animal, you must design the trap on paper; draw a diagram of it. Then write a paragraph describing where the trap will be placed, how it will be set, and how it works. Also include what you learned about the animal that led you to this design. The space below will allow you to develop a rough sketch of your idea.

If your plan is to hunt the animal then you must write a paragraph explaining what the environment of the animal is, what its habits and instincts are and what you are going to do to overcome these advantages in stalking it. Your goal is to develop a plan that will get you within 50 yards of the animal. A picture or series of pictures can accompany this explanation. The space below will allow you to develop a rough sketch of these pictures.

A Rough Sketch of the Trap or Stalking Plan

CHAPTER SEVEN

What the Pioneers Ate and How They Prepared Their Food

Food as Diverse as the Cultures

A good time to introduce the concept of America being a "melting pot" of nationalities would be during this unit. Nothing reflects a person's cultural heritage better than food. Most of what we eat at holidays and even in our week-to-week menus is a reflection of our cultural roots. This was certainly true of the pioneers of the eighteenth and nineteenth centuries. The Scotch-Irish and Pennsylvania Dutch settled into the region west of the Appalachian Mountains. Scandinavian, Swiss, and French settlers moved into the Minnesota and Wisconsin territories. As early as the 1600s, Spanish settlers came to the Southwest. After the Civil War, African-Americans moved into the plains region to establish their own communities. Each culture first brought with them their own beliefs about eating and their own recipes. Frontier living altered some of these habits because the often harsh conditions prevented certain foods from being grown and prepared. In the end each frontier family's menu was a combination of past practice and innovation. Across the time and distance that was our American frontier, great differences occurred in dietary habits. The information in this chapter provides a representative sampling of what the pioneers ate and how they prepared their meals.

Wood for Cooking

Even the first pioneers knew before embarking on their journey that they needed to bring along cooking supplies if they were going to survive. The kettle, a pan, some spoons made of wood or metal, and even a large fork were standard equipment in the traveling bags of those Old West pioneers during the eighteenth century. Those first pioneers used open fires when they arrived at their destination. In constructing a half-faced camp, the open end of the lean-to faced a fire over which was a kettle suspended from a branch supported by two Y-shaped logs. The branch and logs were made of fresh wood so that they did not easily burn when the food was cooking.

ACTIVITY   *Wood That Will Not Burn*

Students have a hard time understanding how pioneers could use wood around a fire when cooking. Allowing students to see a sample of an old, dried piece of wood and a piece of freshly cut wood will help them better understand how wood could be used around fire without burning. A simple experiment will also drive the point home.

Procedure:

1. Place a small piece of dry wood in a Zip-loc plastic bag.
2. Do the same with a piece of freshly cut wood.
3. Put them aside for a day and have students note the moisture that has accumulated in the bag with the fresh piece of wood.

Like most plants, wood contains a great deal of moisture when it is freshly cut. That moisture acts as a natural fire retardant, which is why pioneers could use this wood to support their kettles over a fire.

Once inside the log home, the pioneer still needed fire. The building of a fireplace and chimney were essential. Like their colonial predecessors, the pioneer family of the Eastern Mississippi region and the Pacific Northwest usually had a large fireplace, sometimes taking up the better part of one wall. This provided all the heat for cooking and keeping the home warm. Stones from fields and streams were lugged to the house and placed into position to form the chimney and fireplace. Once an area became somewhat populated, brick that was made in a nearby brick factory might be used. Since this region is richly forested, these pioneers had an abundance of fuel right outside their door.

Innovations With Fuel and Fire

By the later 1800s when the pioneers were moving into the plains regions, cooking technology had sufficiently improved so that cast iron stoves were available. On their prairie schooners they brought with them these stoves. A stove was large, heavy, and unwieldy but well worth the struggle of getting it out west. It provided all the heat of a more traditional fireplace but took up a fraction of the space. Sod homes were typically smaller log houses and space was at a premium. These stoves could be placed more centrally in the house to provide an even heat. The chimney was made of stovepipe that could be linked together and led out of the house through an easily made hole in the sod.

Fuel was another matter entirely for the sod house pioneer. Any available wood was quickly secured in the first years. People traveled up to 40 miles to obtain wood that was not even very good. Pioneers soon learned what the native Americans had known for centuries earlier. Dried buffalo chips (manure) made a surprisingly clean and odorless fuel source, and there were plenty of these to be found all over the prairie for those first settlers. They collected and piled them into ricks to keep them dry. When cattle drives were popular, a homesteader welcomed the trail herd on his open land because of the cow chips they supplied.

Eventually, even this source of fuel became scarce, and once again a new type of fuel was needed. Hay was the next available material. Loose hay burned hot and fast so it had to be twisted into slower-burning bundles. Piles of these hay twists would be stacked in the home to stay dry, leaving little room for anything else. As farmers became more successful at growing corn, another source of fuel was created. Corn cobs or corn stalks banded into logs were used to fuel the stove.

It is obvious that the pioneers had to be innovative and resourceful to keep an adequate fuel supply. Today, our energy demands are met mostly through the use of electricity. Producing this electricity requires the turning of turbines which requires other fuel sources.

Purpose:

The following research project is designed to make students aware of the many fuel sources that exist and to analyze which sources may be best used in the future.

Procedure:

1. Divide students into research teams.
2. Allow students to choose one of these fuel sources to research:

moving water	fossil fuels	tidal power
solar power	– coal	geothermal
nuclear power	– oil	garbage
wind	– natural gas	grain fuels

3. Guide students through their research. The outline below will give them a framework around which to fashion their report.

   A. Where is this fuel source found?
      1. Where is it located in the world?
      2. Is it transportable?
   B. How is this fuel source used?
      1. How is it used in the making of electricity?
      2. Is it used in any other way?
   C. What are the advantages and disadvantages to using this source? Consider the following:
      1. cost
      2. pollution created
      3. reserves available
      4. ability to transport

4. Have students present their information in any way that best suits your class situation. They could develop a traditional report, present the information orally to the class, or develop one chart or a series of charts and diagrams that could be displayed. This could become a bulletin board display, too.

5. By allowing students to share the information, they can begin to formulate opinions regarding which fuel sources should or should not be used. In fact, this sets the groundwork for an in-class debate on the subject with different teams taking opposite sides.

Food for the Pioneer

As mentioned in chapter six, fresh and salted game meat was a chief staple for the pioneer. It got him through tough winters as well as years of poor crop production. Still, the goal of most settlers was to have variety and a lot of it when it came to food. For that reason pioneers made the family garden a part of summer life. From it came the fresh vegetables that could be eaten as they ripened or preserved for winter's use. Common among these garden vegetables were peas (in the cool of the spring), beans, cabbage, okra, turnips, rhubarb, white and sweet potatoes, squash, pumpkin, corn, tomatoes, melons, carrots, and onions, as well as a variety of spices. Today's small suburban gardens are postage-stamp size compared to the large gardens of the early settlers, who relied all year on what they could grow and preserve from the garden.

In addition to growing their food, many pioneers, especially the early ones, adapted to what the region had to offer in the way of wild plants. Foremost among these would have been nuts. Walnuts, chestnuts, pecans, hickory nuts, piñon nuts, and hazel nuts provided a wonderful treat for the drab diet of the early settlers. Even acorns would look good if a family was coming on hard times. Fruits were also available according to their season. There were strawberries, gooseberries, elderberries, red and black raspberries, blackberries, currants, plums, and grapes. Eventually these fruits and others became cultivated. Apples from the East were brought in and grown as well as peaches, pears, and blueberries. All added to the ever-evolving diet of the frontier family.

ACTIVITY   *A Trip to the Grocery*

If the pioneers could be transported to one of our modern-day supermarkets, they would be totally awestruck at the quantity and variety of food available. Instead of foods strictly indigenous to the area, we have foods grown from all over the United States and the world, and we have these foods nearly all year long.

Purpose:

To develop in students an awareness of where the produce they eat originates.

Procedure:

1. Assign students the job of closely investigating the produce department of a local supermarket. If more than one store is available, try to get as many covered as possible. Students are to write the names of all fresh fruits and vegetables that are available. (This would even include varieties such as leaf lettuce, iceberg lettuce, bibb lettuce, etc.)

2. As students are developing this list they must also try to find out from where the fruit or vegetable comes. This is sometimes easily ascertained by looking at the packing boxes used to display the produce. Some produce even have stickers which tell their places of origin. Eventually, however, students will need to speak to a store employee to get all the information. (Store managers will usually be willing to promote their stores by helping out.)

3. Organize the material into a chart and on a map. These can be classroom charts or individual charts. Separate charts for fruits, vegetables, and spices can be made. Each chart should have two or three columns—one for the type of produce, one for the variety, and one for where it was grown. Using a world and U.S. map, have students label where the different types of produce are grown.

   Both the charts and the map can be used as displays.

4. Finally, have students highlight on the chart all the fruits and vegetables that originate in their state or region. With another color have them highlight produce that could be grown in their area but is not.

   Doing this allows students to quickly see how the pioneer's variety of foods was appreciably different from theirs.

5. Have them circle those fruits and vegetables that pioneers living in your area would have had the most success growing in their vegetable garden, assuming they had the seed.

Note: If not everyone can get to a grocery store, divide students into teams with some team members responsible for developing the charts and maps.

Classroom Cooking

Cooking in the classroom is ideal but often not practical. Most of the recipes developed in this section require only a hot plate as a heat source. Toaster ovens or access to a cafeteria oven make some of the recipes easier. If cooking in the classroom is not possible, making it an at-home activity still provides the experience for those involved. Having students bring their creations and heating them will allow students to taste what our pioneer ancestors ate on a regular basis.

Organize

The key to classroom cooking is to be well-organized. Students need to be divided into teams with each team having clearly defined roles. Preview their jobs ahead of time to ensure that things get done right. If your class is large and/or rambunctious, do not try to get everyone involved. With such classes, separate students into groups, with each group having its turn to cook for the other groups. While you work with the cooking group, the rest of the class can do an assignment that does not require supervision. In the end each group takes pride in serving its creation to the rest of the class.

Make it a practice when dealing with food in the classroom to notify parents and inform them of what is on the menu. At this time, mention that if their child has any food allergies they need to inform you so allowances can be made.

Pioneer vs. Modern Cooking

Keep in mind at all times that a pioneer made due with what was available and spent much less time measuring than we do today. The amounts listed in all recipes are guidelines. You will find the recipes rather forgiving. Do not be afraid to cook with instinct. Have students check for doneness themselves and do not rely on the clock. The pioneers certainly did not. After several tries, students will get pretty good at estimating amounts and developing a sense for when things are right.

Also, do not be afraid to make variations. When cooking in class, you might make two versions of the same basic recipe so that students can taste the difference themselves and decide which they would make again if they were colonists.

Since colonists did not always have some ingredients, you may want to improvise as they would have. Some recipes call for sugar. Refined white sugar was just not available for the settlers as it is today. Molasses was what their colonial predecessors relied on but they soon learned to use maple sugar, honey, and sorghum sweetener. You may want, however, to be a bit careful with molasses. Students may think molasses is strong tasting. Honey or maple sugar will be more acceptable to them.

Vegetable Garden Soup

An easy and sure-fire successful cooking experience for the classroom is vegetable soup. It requires little to no culinary skill. It involves a hands-on experience for students and rewards them in the end with an aroma-filled room and a cup of their own creation.

Something that needs to be emphasized to students is the use of meat in any main-dish recipe. Settlers simply were not vegetarians. They relied on game and domestic livestock as an integral part of their diet. A day without meat was certainly not by choice. Therefore, the following recipe although called vegetable soup was really a vegetable beef or a poultry vegetable soup that relied heavily on meat or meat stock as a base.

You can use real meat and meat bones in this recipe if you are interested in authenticity. That requires trimming fat from the meat, cooking it in the water about 1½ hours before adding vegetables and still adding some bouillon to enhance the flavor. I recommend just using bouillon cubes from the beginning to save time and effort. It is one of the few concessions that is worthwhile.

Utensils:

a large pot or several smaller ones with covers
cutting board or cutting surface (cloth covered desks are OK)
butter knives or table knives for cutting vegetables
large long-handled spoon for stirring
heat source such as a hotplate or stovetop
cheesecloth (optional)
colander (optional)
potato peeler (optional)

Ingredients:

Choice of ingredients is entirely up to your discretion. Variety is the spice of life (and soup), so I recommend using as much as is available. Amounts are up to you as noted on the next page.

tomatoes	carrots	potatoes	okra	cabbage
peas	celery	onion	corn	turnips

spices such as bay leaves, allspice, thyme leaves, and peppercorn (use sparingly—only 1 or 2 of each)
about 4–5 bouillon cubes or packets—As it cooks, taste it and if the taste is distinctly weak, add more bouillon.
6–8 quarts of water

Procedure:

1. Prepare meat bones (if you are using them) by trimming off as much fat as possible.

2. Bring water to a boil and put meat bones in the water to boil for about 90 minutes prior to putting in vegetables.

3. Prepare vegetables:
   –Wash them and allow them to drain in colander
   –Peel potatoes, carrots, and turnips. This is really optional. The peelings will not affect taste as long as these root vegetables are well washed.
   –Slice and cube the vegetables. Celery tops are fine to include. You can even buy corn on the cob and give students the job of removing, slicing it from the cob. Tomatoes offer a nice flavor but are a problem because they need peeling and must be scalded in hot water to loosen the peels.

4. Toss it all in the boiling water and let it simmer for between 1–2 hours (longer if necessary.) Employ a "tasting crew" to let everyone know when it is done.

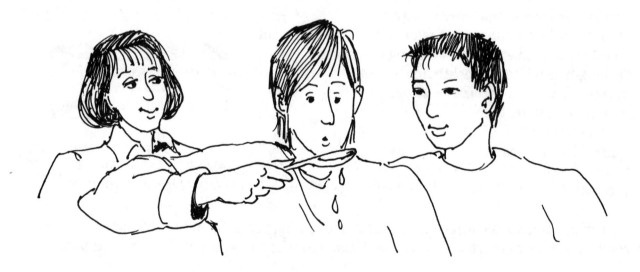

General Notes and Tips for Soup Making

- There are no required amounts for the vegetables. A few more carrots, a few less stalks of celery more or less has no real effect on the recipe. The more you add the more stew-like the soup becomes. You must, however, make enough for each student to have about a cup's worth. Plan on making the recipe in a large (16-quart) pot or several smaller ones depending on what kind of heat source is available.

Notes (Continued)

- Potatoes will have a thickening effect on the broth as starch from the potatoes is released. Navy beans in the soup are realistic since pioneers relied heavily on this easy-to-grow vegetable. I have found, however, that too many students shy away from bean-style soup to make it a practical cooking experience, but you can make that judgment based on your own class. Rice or noodles make even better soup, but in all honesty only the most established settlers living near a town had access to those items.

- This activity does require more time than is found in a single 45-55 minute period. Consequently, you may need to divide the process between two days. It is most effective, however, if students cannot only do the preparation, but be present during the cooking that leads to the eating.

- The spices mentioned below can be simply dropped into the soup or wrapped in cheese cloth. If you drop them in, tell students not to eat or they will be in for a sharp-tasting and eye-watering experience.

- The vegetables can be handled a number of ways. They can be cleaned, prepared, and sliced by students right in class. I have always preferred that method. For a neater more antiseptic approach you can also have students do all the preparation and slicing of vegetables at home and have them bring them to class in plastic bags.

- It is nice to have something to eat with the soup. The bread recipe on page 84 can be prepared in advance and saved until the soup is made. In fact, you can have one group of students make bread while others make soup. That undertaking may need an extra adult supervisor if both are going on at the same time.

- Finally, as the soup simmers you may lose more water than you anticipated. Do not be afraid to add more as you go along to avoid the much less popular vegetable-mush stew.

Johnnycake

So, who is Johnny and why did they name a cake after him? That seems like the logical question to ask but in reality johnnycake is named after no one. The word is a derivation of the words *journey cake*. It is a cornmeal-based cake. These small cakes were ideal for travel whereby they got their original name of *journey cake*. Eventually the *r* got lost in the pronunciation and it wasn't long before an *h* was added to the spelling giving it its present-day misnomer.

The first johnnycake was strictly a corn bread attempt at making the breads the colonists relished back in England. One real important difference, however, made corn unsuitable for rising since it had no gluten. *Gluten* is a protein that gives raw dough its elasticity and holds in the CO_2 produced by yeasts. Thus, wheat bread with gluten will inflate (rise) but a corn dough mixture allows the CO_2 to escape, thus no rising.

Another characteristic of this first corn bread was its crumbly nature. Both these "problems" were eventually solved by adding a little wheat or rye flour to the mixture, both of which have gluten. Although the rising was not as pronounced, the crumbly nature of the bread lessened. The recipe below is the "improved" version with wheat flour. You may, however, want to try out the more original johnnycake recipe by leaving out the wheat flour. When you are done you will have what the Indians called *corn pone*.

Ingredients:

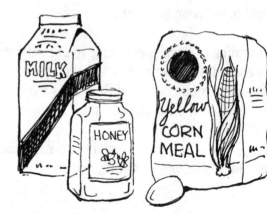

1 cup all-purpose flour
a little over 1 cup cornmeal (white or yellow)
2 tsp. baking powder
2 Tbs. sweetener (honey, molasses, or sugar)
1 tsp. salt
1 egg
3 Tbs. melted butter or bacon drippings
1 cup milk

Procedure:

1. Mix the dry ingredients together in a separate bowl.
2. Blend the liquid ingredients in another bowl.
3. Combine liquid and wet ingredients in a few strokes, don't overdo it.
4. Place the batter in a greased skillet and cover it. Cook it for about 30 minutes on a low/medium heat covered. Check it for doneness, occasionally checking to see that it is not burning on the bottom.
   Or, Pour small portions onto a griddle and cook them like pancakes.

Variations:

You can add anything you like to the mixture. Make it hardy with nuts or cooked meats. Make it dessert-like with raisins or dried fruits or let students decide.

 FS-10140 Life as a Pioneer

Flapjacks

This American breakfast item had its roots in most European countries, was brought with the immigrants, and then adapted to the pioneer setting. The Germans called them *blintzes,* the French called them *crepes,* and the Austrians named them *nockerln*. They are also called *pancakes, griddle cakes,* and *wheat cakes.*

The premise behind the making of flapjacks is simple. Develop a batter with milk and flour that is thin enough to be poured and cook it on a very hot griddle or pan so that it cooks completely in only a few minutes. Today's recipes often come from a box of prepared dry batter, but this was not available for the pioneer.

The two recipes below will result in edible flapjacks and help students to realize how adaptable cooking had to be for the pioneer. Both recipes will require a hotplate type heat source and pan or a griddle. If it does not have a nonstick finish, you will need to grease it with butter beforehand. The amounts shown are for a simple recipe that makes 10–15 three-inch flapjacks. Double or triple the recipe as needed.

Ingredients Have Changed

The below recipes are not completely authentic because the ingredients are not available as they were 150 years ago. The first recipe calls for sour milk. Real sour milk can only be made from unpasteurized milk. If pasteurized milk is allowed to sour it just spoils. Buttermilk could be used as a substitute. Unfortunately, real buttermilk is nothing like what we buy today in the store. Real buttermilk is what is left over after the milk has been churned into butter. It has little fat and has a watery consistency. Today's manufactured buttermilk is doctored up with cultures to thicken it and butter particles to richen it. So, where does that leave the recipe? The closest substitute I can suggest is skim milk. The dry bread pieces in the recipe can be saved at home by students and brought to class.

Waste Nothing Flapjacks

The pioneers wasted little of what they made. The recipe below illustrates how left-over dry bread could be used as a base for delicious flapjacks

Ingredients:

dry bread pieces
2 cups skim milk
1 egg
a pinch of salt
white flour
1 tsp. of baking powder

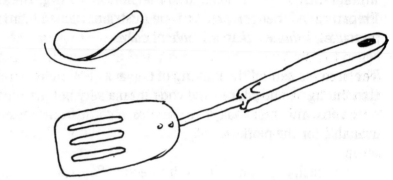

Procedure:

1. Soak the dry bread pieces in the skim milk until they are soft and then break them up into a thick mixture. It may still be lumpy.
2. To this mixture add salt, egg, baking powder, and enough flour to create the thick pancake consistency you want.
3. Toast on the hot griddle until it bubbles, then flip them and toast them on the other side. Serve with maple syrup

Corn Flapjacks

Until settlers became established throughout Kansas and Nebraska and began growing wheat in abundance, the grain that most pioneers relied on was corn. Corn lacked the gluten found in wheat flour that allows bread to rise when yeast is added, and it could not be ground as fine as wheat. Nonetheless, it was a staple in every meal. The below recipe still requires a little wheat flour but it is used sparingly as the pioneers would.

Ingredients:

1⅓ cups cornmeal
¼ cup white flour
1 tsp. salt
½ tsp. baking soda
¼ cup softened butter
2 cups skim milk
2 eggs

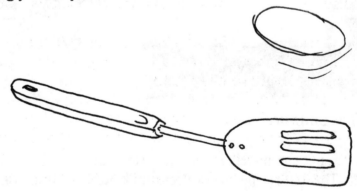

Procedure:

1. Mix the dry ingredients and then add the rest of the ingredients to create a thick flapjack consistency. Add more flour or milk as needed. A few strokes is all that is needed.
2. Toast on the hot griddle until it bubbles, then flip them and toast them on the other side. Serve with maple syrup.

Maple Syrup

Unlike the colonists of the 17th century who relied on molasses for their sweetening, the pioneers of the 18th and 19th century relied on honey and maple syrup to satisfy their sweet tooth. "Sugaring-off" was the name that the pioneers gave to the process of obtaining maple syrup from the sap of the sugar maple or the black maple tree. In March when the sap of the maple tree began to flow brought on by warm days and cold nights, the settler tapped the tree about about 4 feet from the ground using a small auger. Spiles, hollow round tubes, were driven about an inch into the trunk and sap ran through these spiles and into a bucket or a trough. Gallons of the sap were collected and brought to a central location where it was poured into a huge kettle and boiled down into the consistency of syrup. It took about 30 gallons of sap to produce one gallon of maple syrup.

Making Maple Syrup–A Simulation

The sap from a maple tree does not taste sweet when it comes right from the tree. That's because it is less than 2% "sugar." The process of boiling it down took hours and hours. During this time the pioneer had to stir it frequently to keep it from burning and skim it just as often to remove the ash and bits of dirt that would inevitably get into the kettle. The following activity allows students to appreciate how much time went into the process.

Purpose:

To simulate the boiling down part of sugaring-off.

Procedure:

1. Add one tablespoon of refined white sugar to 1 or 1-1/2 quarts of water and stir until it is totally dissolved.
2. Allow a student or two to taste it to verify that it is only slightly sweet. Have them do this intermittenly during the process to see how it is getting sweeter and sweeter.
3. Put this water in a pot and bring it to a full boil.
4. Continue boiling this mixture until it boils down to a syrupy consistency. This will take a while and will result in only about 2-3 tablespoons of syrup. It must be attended and constantly stirred near the end to prevent burning. Students will be amazed at how little syrup results from so much liquid.
5. Add a few drops of artificial maple flavor during the process to better simulate the sugaring-off smell.

By allowing it to further evaporate and cool a hard maple sugar was created that could be used in cooking.

Apples

"As American as apple pie" is an expression that is more myth than truth. Your students may be interested in knowing that when the first colonists arrived in America there were only four varieties of crab apples indigenous to America. What the English, French, and Dutch colonists soon realized, however, is that the proper climate existed in America for the cultivation of a good apple harvest. It was they who brought the seeds from Europe that grew into the apple industry that we have today.

The pioneers recognized the usefulness of apple orchards for their farm. They provided a food product that was sweet and nutritious and could be preserved a number of ways to get them through the winter. The trees, when planted correctly, provided a windbreak for the house, the pasture, or any other part of the farm. Seedlings were actually packed into the covered wagons and planted soon after arrival at the new homestead.

General Recipe Notes

The recipes below are simple and accommodate a class of students. The baked apples require an oven. The applesauce and apple fritters can use a hot plate or stove top. Preparing apples is an activity that students will genuinely enjoy. See if anyone has an apple corer at home. It saves time. If not, table knives or butter knives will do the trick. Apples need to be cored and peeled. In the apple fritter and baked apple recipe, you will want to keep the apples from getting brown after they are peeled and sliced. To do this, have students place peeled slices into a pot of cold water until they are to be used. The aroma of cooking apples will get everyone anxious to taste what is being cooked.

Baked Apples

Ingredients and Utensils:

½ to 1 apple per student
brown sugar and cinnamon to the ratio of 5:1.
raisins or sliced almonds (optional)
butter
baking pan
butter or table knives

Procedure:

1. Students dig out the core from the apple to about ½ inch from the bottom. Do not peel the apples.

2. Mix the brown sugar, cinnamon, raisins, and nuts together and fill the core with this mixture.

3. Put a pat of butter on the top.

4. Place the apples on the baking pan and cover the bottom of the pan with water.

5. Bake the apples at 375° for 45 minutes to an hour. They should be soft but not mushy. Be careful! They will be very hot at first.

Applesauce

Ingredients and Utensils:

about 1 apple per student
sugar (to taste)
cinnamon
water
pot
butter knives or table knives
stirring spoon

Procedure:

1. Students core and peel and cut the apples into pieces. You may choose to leave the peels on and remove most of them after cooking. This will give your applesauce a red color.

2. Put the apples into the pot and cover with water. Simmer the apples until very tender.

3. Remove and mash them up or blend them. An old-fashioned potato masher works fine.

4. Add sugar to taste. Some apples are sweeter than others to begin with so this will take a little testing.

5. Cook gently for a few more minutes and either serve warm or allow to cool. Sprinkle a little cinnamon on top before eating.

Apple Fritters

Ingredients and Utensils:

The following ingredient amounts will make enough dough so that every student in the class has one fritter. Increase the recipe proportionately if you want more.

4 eggs
1½ cup milk
2 Tbs. melted butter
2 cups flour
½ tsp. salt
2 Tbs. sugar
cooking oil
confectioner's sugar
mixing bowl
mixing spoon
tongs
butter knives or tables knives

Procedure:

1. Mix the first set of ingredients together. It would be best to do this one day and refrigerate it. Then do the cooking the next day. This ensures that the dough will develop the consistency necessary to stick to the apples. It is not absolutely necessary.

2. Students peel and core the apples and cut them into rings.

3. Heat about an inch of cooking oil in the pan. It is hot enough when a drop of dough put in the oil bubbles and fries immediately.

4. Pat dry the slices of apple and dust them with confectioner's sugar.

5. Dip the slices into the batter and place in the hot oil. Cook until brown on one side, then turn them and cook them on the other side.

6. Remove them from the oil and drain on a paper towel before eating. Be careful! They will be hot inside. You can also dust the finished fritter with confectioner's sugar.

CHAPTER EIGHT

Health and Medicine

Sanitation and the Pioneer

If ever there were an example of survival of the fittest, it was the early pioneers. Those that were not rugged and healthy were quickly weeded out by the extreme conditions under which the pioneers lived. Disease, fever, and skin sores were a way of life, and those unable to tolerate these conditions either gave up and left or gave out and died. Pioneers knew little of the sanitary conditions we expect in our homes and public places today. They understood even less about the relationship between these conditions and their general health. Even if they had understood, however, it is unlikely that they would have done much about it. The raw life of a pioneer did not lend itself to the comparatively sterile lives we live today.

Poverty conditions contributed to a life style lacking cleanliness. Clothes were seldom washed owing to the fact that the outfit being worn was all that was owned. As settlements became more populated, more clothing was available, but work clothes were still worn for days or weeks on end before being cleaned. That meant that the mud from the pasture and the manure from the barnyard were brought into the house with the farmer. Shoes were a luxury for many early pioneers. Barefoot was the norm leaving the many settlers open to a variety of infections when the foot was scratched or punctured.

Sanitation (continued)

Bathing was infrequent. In summer months warm weather allowed bathing in the river or pond, but since cleanliness was not a habit, fewer than expected took advantage of the situation. Bathing in the winter required the use of a kettle to heat water. Since the one and only kettle a pioneer family might own was used constantly to prepare meals, weeks or months could go by before a full bath was ambitiously undertaken. Daily washing consisted of a basin kept by a fire that everyone used to rinse grime or grit from their faces and hands. Dirt floors in log cabins, dirt walls and ceilings in sod houses, along with manure and mud being tracked in daily led to an unavoidable layer of dirt that coated everything and everyone.

Dirt alone, of course, does not cause disease. The microorganisms sustained in the dirt do. Dirty hands rubbing eyes, dirt worked into cuts and scratches, and insects such as mites, ticks, and fleas that come with the dirt helped initiate illness among pioneers. Communal living is what spread it. Water was brought in from a creek or pond and placed in a pitcher. A common gourd might be used to dip water out when anyone was thirsty. A common towel was used to dry faces and hands after washing up in the basin that everyone else had used. In fact, everything was shared among family members to get its fullest use but little was washed between uses. In prairie towns that relied on the same source for its water supply, a disease could sweep through an entire settlement in a matter of days. Close living conditions also promoted the spread of airborne disease in cabins and sod houses.

Even today, students contract most of their diseases through careless contact with others who are infected with an illness. In the classroom microorganisms are spread primarily in an airborne manner when infected students talk, sneeze, or cough so close to others that the microorganisms are inhaled. Another culprit in the spread of diseases is the sharing of foods. Still another is the spread of microorganisms via touching (e.g., an ill student coughs on his/her hand then touches another student's hand who in turn touches his/her eye, etc.). This process of germ spreading can be demonstrated to students in the following exercise.

92

ACTIVITY *Germ Tag*

Purpose:

To demonstrate to students how easily germs can be spread among people who must live or work closely together.

Procedure:

1. The teacher decides which student will be "it." This should be someone in class who is in good health.

2. Contact this person privately and inform them that it is their job to "infect" as many classmates as possible within a given amount of time. For example, if you teach in a self-contained classroom the time might be half a day. In a class that meets once a day it might be two class periods.

3. Do not tell the class who is "it" and do not tell the class that a game is even being played. No one except the infector and the teacher should know what is going on.

4. Explain that they can "infect" students in several ways:

   a. via face-to-face conversation (airborne)

   b. sitting next to them (airborne)

   c. by sharing something like a pencil (touching)

   d. by direct contact such as a handshake (touching)

   Note: Although sharing food is a very real and common method of passing illnesses, this should not be encouraged during the game.

5. During the time limit, the person who is it should keep a log of who is infected and in what manner.

6. When the time is elapsed, inform the class what has been going on. Introduce the infector and have students stand who think they might have become infected. Then have the infector share his/her results.

Variations:

1. Play the game a second time with a secret infector, but since students know that someone is out to infect them have them note how their behavior changes. Have students keep a log of ways that they avoided contact with everyone.

2. Have the infector keep a chart. In one column are those he "Definitely Infected" by talking to them face to face or by touching their hands. The next column are those he "Likely Infected" by sitting next to them. The last column is those he "Possibly Infected" by sharing an object like a pencil.

Insects and Disease

Insects were mercilessly present at all times. In the summer months flies and mosquitoes dominated. Manure piles and outhouses attracted the flies which then invaded the kitchen and milking areas. Dead flies would fall in the milk pails, live ones alighted on food and covered fruits and vegetables that were being dried for winter use. Each fly carried with it the potential spread of microorganisms. Mosquitoes were viewed as a bigger nuisance. Spring rains and melting snows soaked the ground and allowed pools of stagnant water to develop. It was here that the female anopheles mosquito bred and released the horde that infected pioneers with the *ague*, also known as *malaria*.

ACTIVITY   *Germs Transferred From Flies*

Nearly everyone has had the experience of trying to brush away an annoying fly during a picnic. Besides being a buzzing annoyance, flies are carriers of bacteria that can infest our food supply. Students can see what happens when the microbes that are already on a fly are allowed to grow.

Purpose:

To demonstrate to students how the bacteria found on flies can be transferred to food.

Materials:

tomato soup	large spoon	boiling water
2 containers	plastic wrap	one dead fly
hot plate	rubber bands	

Procedure:

1. Sterilize the containers and spoon in boiling water.

2. Bring the tomato soup to a boil.

3. Pour some hot soup into the first container. Cover it with plastic wrap immediately and secure with a rubber band.

4. Follow the same procedure for the other container but add a dead fly to the mixture.

5. Put containers in a warm, dark place and chart the growth of mold daily. Students can record data and draw conclusions about the presence of microorganisms in their environment.

A white mold should begin to develop in the container with the fly. In the other container no mold should develop since it was covered before it could become contaminated. The bacteria on the fly uses the tomato soup as a medium for growth. When a fly lands on food we eat that same transfer of bacteria occurs.

Variation:

If you do not want to go to all the trouble of boiling soup, you can still grow the mold by placing the dead fly in a dish of water and covering it with plastic wrap. Although this does not provide a food medium nor a comparison to a germ free dish, it does still show the growth of mold from the bacteria on a fly.

Food Storage and Health

Inadequate food storage also promoted disease. As mentioned above, flies and other insects could easily invade a larder or root cellar. Freezing fresh meat was possible during winter months when the temperatures did not go above freezing, but during the rest of the year, meat had to be dried or salted to be preserved. Freshly slaughtered animal meat went bad in a day's time, but the pioneer family would not consider throwing away food. Consequently, rancid meat or dairy products were doctored up with spices or cooked as is, leaving settlers open to a variety of illnesses caused by eating spoiled food.

Pioneers avoided the decay of foods through preservation methods still employed today. These include drying, pickling, and refrigeration. Moisture is one of the key ingredients needed for molds to grow. By reducing the moisture in meats, fruits, and vegetables, they effectively reduced the chance of spoilage due to growing molds. Likewise, pickling the foods reduced mold growth since molds and bacteria do not grow well in the acidic (vinegar) and salty solution used in pickling. Finally, pioneers learned that the cool water of springs and wells retarded the spoilage of foods that were lowered into these natural refrigerators. Over time a settler might add a spring house to his homestead. This was a small shack located over a stream or spring. Foods that needed preserving were tied in a bundle and lowered into the cool water where the lower temperature reduced bacterial growth.

ACTIVITY *Preserving Foods*

Purpose:

To observe the effects of refrigeration, drying, and pickling on the growth of bacteria and molds.

Materials:

4 dishes	salt	2 bouillon cubes	dry cereal
2 glasses	vinegar	2 bread slices	water
plastic wrap		rubber bands	

Procedure:

Drying Foods

1. In two of the dishes place some dry cereal. In both dishes sprinkle some dust from the classroom or dirt from outside.

2. In one of the two dishes add enough water to thoroughly soak the cereal.

3. Cover both with plastic wrap and secure with a rubber band. Place them both in a warm, dark place.

Refrigeration

4. Take the bread slices and wipe them on the floor. Place each in its own dish and sprinkle with water.

5. Cover both with plastic wrap and secure with a rubber band. Place one in a warm, dark place and the other in a refrigerator.

Pickling

6. Dissolve the bouillon cubes in two cups of boiling water.

7. Divide this solution between two clean glasses.

8. In one of the glasses add a teaspoon of salt and three teaspoons of vinegar. Mix well. Allow them to cool.

9. To both sprinkle in a little dirt or dust.

10. Cover both with plastic wrap and secure with a rubber band. Place them both in a warm, dark place.

These three experiments will allow students to see the effects of these three preservative techniques. Students should do daily observations for no more than a week to note the growth of molds or bacteria.

The dry cereal should not grow any mold at all unless moisture gets into the dish. This illustrates why the pioneers went to such great lengths to dry fruits, vegetables, and meats.

The refrigerated bread may grow mold, but it should occur after the growth of mold on the other bread sample has begun.

Mold growth in the bouillon water will be noted by a cloudiness of the water. The vinegar and salt should slow down this process in the other glass.

Folk Medicine or Folk Tales?

Folk medicine is the name given to medical practices that have been handed down from one generation to the next but carry little or no scientific research to support them. This is not to say that these practices were all hokum. Unfortunately, some were. Others, however, did work and only later did scientific investigation discover what chemical contained in the plant provided the cure.

Without the opportunity to reach a doctor and with little or no formal education, pioneers relied on cures that they learned from their own parents or on the folk remedies of a neighboring "expert." Most of these cures involved plants found naturally in the forests, pastures, and swamps of the area. Often families would bring the seeds of these herbs with them as they traveled west. Once a garden could be established, these seeds were used to grow the herbs that they believed would bring relief from aches, pains, and fevers.

Each herb had its special use. The root, stem, leaves, or flowers could be used depending on the plant. In some cases a tea was brewed from plant parts. Another method was to boil the plant or plant part and mash it into a paste which could then be made into a poultice (i.e., a soft sticky mixture that is heated and spread on a cloth and applied to the skin).

A good many of these homemade cures were simply useless. For example the plant commonly called "forget-me-not" was thought to bring courage and/or increase one's memory. Sorry, this just does not happen no matter how the herb is taken. On the other hand, many settlers believed fresh greens made into a "spring tonic" could tighten loose teeth. This was not so far-fetched. Loose teeth are a symptom of scurvy, a condition caused by a diet lacking in vitamin C. As winter months progressed and the pioneer diet relied more and more on meat and dried foods and less and less on fresh greens this condition would begin to manifest itself. When spring arrived and teas made from fresh greens could be made, it is entirely possible that the missing vitamin C was replenished and the gums strengthened. Another plant, called *cinquefoil* for its five-lobed leaves, carries the latin name *potentilla*. This plant is common in perennial gardens for its bright yellow flowers. Scientists know that *potentilla* is the source of a chemical that helps to control muscle spasms.

sage

forget-me-not

potentilla

Real Uses for Herbs

The effect that these teas, poultices, and balms had on the body were many times positive in a general way. Below is a list of uses that these herbs served.

Antiseptic—any herb that kill germs and bacteria

Cathartic—an herb that thoroughly cleaned out the digestive system

Diuretic—an herb that removed water from the body usually via the urinary tract

Laxative—any herb acting as a mild cathartic

Sedative—an herb that induces sleep or a relaxed state

Styptic—any herb that is usually applied to the skin to stop bleeding

Students can easily see how these herbs would be useful. For example, if a pioneer ate some food that had spoiled to such a degree that it was making him ill, then an herb with laxative or cathartic abilities could be employed to help rid the body of the contaminated food. Styptic herbs would be used as a first-aid measure to reduce bleeding for pioneers who cut or punctured themselves. Allow students to come up with other possible ways an herb could be used if it had one of these effects.

The fact that some herbs had these qualities is not in doubt. The belief that some herbs act as magical cures is where folk *medicine* becomes *folk tale*.

Whether your students are in a rural, suburban, or urban environment, it is easy to find herbs used by pioneers. Some herbs grow well in urban settings which afford them more sun and warmth (reflected off the buildings). They can be found in alleys, growing out of sidewalk cracks, and in vacant lots. In more rural settings, whole pastures or woodland areas can become overrun with spreading herbs that thrive because of the right conditions. Students who previously only saw weeds can begin to see herbs with a little bit of research and knowledge.

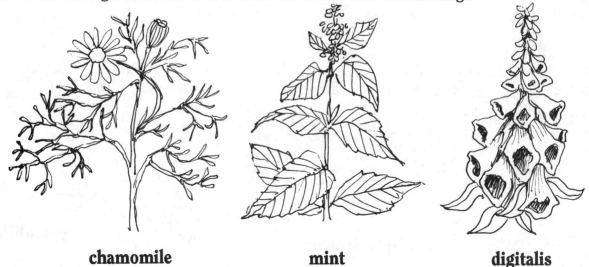

chamomile   **mint**   **digitalis**

                   FS-10140 Life as a Pioneer

Activity—Weed or Herb?

First of all students will need a book that helps them identify herbs and plants. This book needs to be available in the classroom. This project is best done in the autumn or spring when plants are typically blooming so that they can be identified.

Purpose:

To identify some of the herbs that grow naturally in a given area.

Procedure:

1. Working individually or in teams, have students begin to bring in samples of plants found naturally in your area. They should be instructed to look in vacant lots, pastures, roadsides, sidewalk cracks, and their own lawns. Tell them to look for "weeds."
2. Using the book you have obtained for plant identification, allow students to name the plants they have brought in. Accuracy is a goal but in many cases is impossible. Therefore, you may want students to code their identifications according to how certain they are about them. Dry and press the plant by placing it between a few sheets of newspaper and putting a heavy book atop it in a warm place for a few days.
4. Mount the dried plant on art paper and label it with its common name and latin name. If room permits and if you have the information available, a short paragraph about the herb can be attached.
5. Display these mountings.

Success is easy with this activity because there are so many plants spread throughout the United States that were used for medicine, food, or household use. Below is a list of plants that students may easily find no matter where they are located in the United States.

dandelion	sassafras	mint (many varieties)
goldenrod	willow (a tree)	chicory
thistle	yarrow	cattails

Although many students see these plants every day, they seldom consider they could be useful. A project such as the one described on this page will sharpen their awareness of how useful ordinary weeds can be.

CHAPTER NINE
Making a Living

Agriculture

For the pioneer who was part of the first wave of settlers into a frontier area, there was only one thought of how to make a living, farming. Many of the early pioneers came from families who were farmers. Free or inexpensive land, the hope of a better life, or a chance to make their fortune all beckoned these pioneers to try their hand at doing what they knew best. For emigrants from the South, the hope of developing land with tobacco or cotton crops and becoming as wealthy as some of the plantation owners led them first into Kentucky, then Tennessee, and eventually into Arkansas, Mississippi, and Texas. The Easterners and later those from Ohio, Indiana, and Michigan sought to grow wheat knowing full well that back East the cities could buy all the wheat they could furnish. They moved into Iowa and Missouri in the second and third quarters of the nineteenth century and had much more luck with corn. Eventually, as technology and travel improved, Kansas, Nebraska, and the Dakotas became targets of emigrants looking to make their fortune with wheat. We know that wheat did eventually become the crop of these states but it took some hard years and a fair portion of failure before farmers learned to coax wheat out of those fertile but dry plains.

Plowing the Fields

All the early pioneers had to be farmers. The first year or two was spent clearing land and building a house. Setting up a homestead meant building a barn or shed, establishing a vegetable garden, as well as planting enough corn and other grains that would help the frontier farmer survive the winters. For many pioneers, growing just enough to live on was all they wanted or all they could realistically achieve. Some settlers, however, ambitiously wanted more. They wanted to grow a crop that they could sell to buyers, who would then transport the crop to the ever-growing, ever-hungry cities back East. Of all the grains, wheat was the most in demand, but it was also the crop that depended the most on favorable weather conditions and efficient equipment. The United States was strongly dependent on agriculture, and consequently, innovation in agricultural machinery followed.

At first, many farmers worked together as a team helping to plow one another's land, since it often took two men to handle the plow as it turned over the prairie grass. The demand for tools and machinery which would make it possible for one farmer (even one farmer with several strapping sons) to produce more than his family needed grew as fast as pioneers moved westward. Planting wheat, oats, rye, or any small-grain crop required specific steps.

First, a farmer had to turn over the soil with a plow. Early plows were made mostly of wood with iron shares and wooden moldboards (see illustration below). Even when the moldboard was stripped with metal, it still had one major problem with the prairie grasses and forestland roots. The problem was clogging. Every few feet a farmer had to stop and remove the clumps of root-matted soil that encrusted the plowshare. The first innovation to significantly handle that problem was John Deere's steel plow. In 1838 John Deere, along with Leonard Andrus, invented a self-cleaning, steel-bladed plow by welding steel to the wrought iron moldboard. The smooth steel did not clog up and cut through the sod so easily that it was called the *singing plow*. It made it possible for one man and one team of oxen to plow a field alone. By 1847 John Deere made the first all-steel plowshare by beating a circular saw blade into that easily identifiable, curved shape of the plow blade.

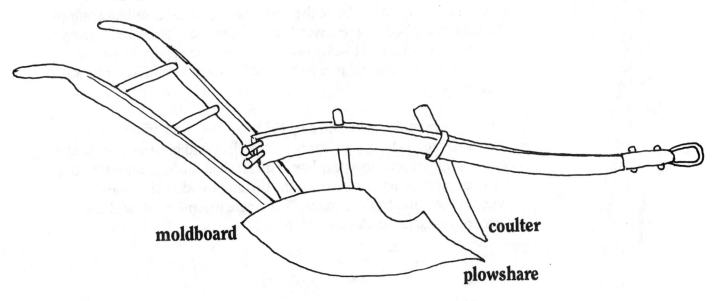

moldboard   coulter

plowshare

Harrowing the Fields

Once the field had been turned over by the plow, it had to be cultivated and leveled for planting. This required an instrument called a *harrow*. One common harrow was made of hardwood and shaped like an *A*. It had long metal teeth and was dragged behind the oxen team.

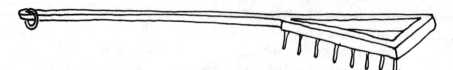

As the oxen pulled the harrow, someone, usually children or the farmer's wife, followed and planted the seeds. East of the one-hundredth meridian, rainfall was plentiful enough to supply water for the crop. Even if it weren't, many farmers settled on land near a creek or pond that would supply irrigation water in times of drought. Beyond the one-hundredth meridian, irrigation was needed regularly. We now know that a tremendous amount of water exists below the surface throughout the central United States. Getting that water, which in some areas was 200 or more feet below the surface, required another agricultural innovation, the windmill.

Irrigation

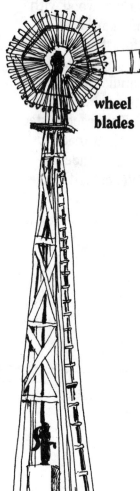

wheel
blades

There were no easy ways to secure a well on one's property, outside of luck. Some men used an auger with attachments to search for water within 20 feet of the surface. Others relied on divining. *Diviners* were people who walked around an area of land with a Y-shaped stick. Holding the ends of the Y, the diviner waited until the end was magically pulled downward via some inexplicable attraction to the water. Sometimes it worked and often it did not.

Once the spot was located, the farmer would get to the backbreaking chore of digging, risking death should a cave-in occur before he reached the water table. Once the well was dug, buckets or hand pumps were put into place for retrieving the water. In the high plains, however, hand pumps will not get water from such extreme depths. What was needed was a mechanical pump that had the force to pull water up such great distances.

The first windmill was invented by 1854 by a New Englander named Daniel Halladay. His design was fairly simple. Wind blew wooden blades which were attached to a gear box. A metal shaft leading down into the well was pumped up and down by the turning wooden blades and brought the water to the surface. This single invention allowed the farmer to irrigate hundreds of dry acres.

Harvesting

Unlike corn, which is considerably easier to harvest, small-grain crops need to be mowed. The first tool used by pioneers was really a very old tool. It was the *scythe*. The scythe is actually a tool dating back to pre-colonial times in Europe. What was done to the scythe for the American farmer was make it better. The scythes of the colonists had a shallow S curved handle that ended in a straight blade running perpendicular to the handle. A shoulder strap was often attached to take up some of the weight of the tool since a farmer might have spent a whole day swinging the thing. (See illustration A.)

One of the first improvements was the addition of a handle grip which gave the farmer better control and leverage. (illustration B) Since cut wheat had to be put in piles, the next improvement provided a way for the farmer to not only make a cut but to also place the cut wheat in a pile without releasing the scythe. This scythe was called a cradle and could have three or four "fingers" on it. (illustration C)

About the time John Deere was making steel plows for farmers in his area, Cyrus McCormick had invented and was producing a mechanical reaper. Drawn by two horses, this machine cut the grain and laid it out neatly so that another man riding along could easily bundle it. The result was a machine that could cut an acre of wheat faster than 20 men could cut with scythes. Eventually, Cyrus McCormick improved on this invention by adding rakes and binders to the reaper to further reduce the amount of work involved in the process.

Once the grain was harvested, the grain had to be separated from the stalk, and then the actual seed had to be separated from the husk or chaff. The first job was called *threshing*. It was traditionally performed by beating the wheat with a tool called a *flail* as the wheat lay on the barn floor. (illustration D) By far, it was one of the more labor intensive jobs involved in the growing and harvesting of wheat. To reduce the work involved, a mechanical thresher was invented in the early 1830s that used the power of horses walking on a treadmill. The stalk (straw) was separated from the grain, moved along a conveyor, and piled in one spot while the grain was sifted into a bag. No flailing for hours on end, no raking, and no sweeping and bagging.

All these agricultural innovations made it possible for a farmer to go beyond subsistence farming and produce crops which could be sold for profit.

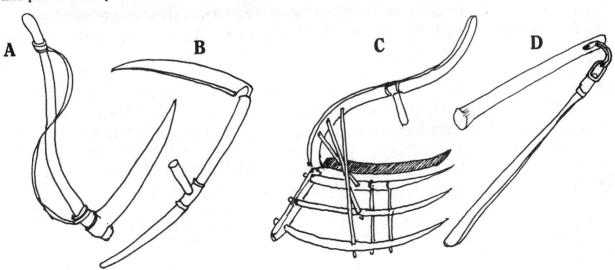

A   B   C   D

The pioneer farmer knew that there was money to be made in wheat. Rye, oats, barley, and corn were fine, but real money could be made by selling wheat that would end up back East. Things are not much different today. Wheat is the principal ingredient in scores of foods that students eat today. The below activity will allow students to investigate how wheat is used in many of the foods they eat.

Purpose:
Students will become aware of the many foods that rely on wheat as an ingredient.

Note:
This activity can be done by students individually or in teams. Students do this activity best if given a few days to finish it.

Procedure:
1. Begin by providing instruction for students on how to read the ingredient panel of a food container. Point out that wheat appears on the list in a number of ways including flour, wheat flour, bleached or unbleached flour, durham flour, and enriched flour. Point out also that ingredients are listed in order of amounts contained in the food product.

2. Tell students (or teams) that their goal is to provide a long list of food items that contain wheat. You can limit it to at-home work or open it up to after school grocery store expeditions. To avoid redundancy within a student's or team's list provide certain limitations such as not listing different brands of the same food product as separate entries.

3. Lists should be numbered for easy count. It is up to you if you want to include a prize for the student or team with the longest list.

4. Discussion can center on any of the following:
   a. Which food products unexpectedly contained wheat?
   b. Which foods used wheat as a main ingredient?
   c. Which foods did not specifically list wheat but definitely used wheat? (e.g. noodle soup only lists noodles but all noodles use wheat flour.)

ACTIVITY *Breakfast Grains*

A popular breakfast food is cereal. The pioneers did not eat as much cereal as we do and certainly not for breakfast. Corn mush was about the most popular grain-type breakfast food during that time period. Today we have dozens of different grain breakfast foods.

Purpose:

To allow students to compare and contrast breakfast cereals and reach conclusions about each.

Procedure:

1. Working individually or in teams, have students make a chart of breakfast cereals. They can rely on their home supply or visit a grocery store to get information. The chart setup would look like this:

Name of Cereal	Grains in Cereal	Other Ingredients
(example) Munchy Pops	corn, wheat, oats	sugar, raisins

2. These results can be transferred to a class chart for comparisons and be used as data for an individual or team report. Things to consider include:
   a grains used most
   b. grains used least
   c. sugared and sugarless cereals
   d. cereals with greatest variety of grains
   e cereals containing one grain variety
   f. cereals professing to be "natural" or "nutritious" which have sugar as a main ingredient. (Remember that corn syrup is a sugar.)

3. The data can then be used to draw conclusions about the most healthy cereals available. On the other hand, students could also devise a "hit list" of cereals to avoid.

Supplemental Activity:

Have students bring in samples of cereals and compose a team of judges who will rate the cereals according to taste alone, then nutritional value.

You may also want to cook up some corn mush (the native Americans called it *corn pone*). Just mix one cup of cornmeal with one cup of water and one teaspoon of salt. Add this mixture to four cups of boiling water. Cook it until it is the right consistency. Serve with molasses, maple syrup, or honey. Let students see for themselves what the pioneer ate as a staple cereal.

When a farmer needed a tool or some equipment, he did not always go out and buy it. In fact, currency as we know it was nowhere near as popular then as now. Farmers who brought their grains to market would often receive goods in return, not money. This bartering system made for some very inexact figuring of what the grain was worth. To one farmer a sack of grain might be equal to a bolt of cloth but to another it was worth a shovel. Giving students the feel for bartering can be done in the classroom.

Purpose:

To have students estimate the value of items through a simulated bartering session.

Procedure:

1. Have students make a list of personal items they have that they believe have barter value. Their list might include: bikes, CDs or tapes, video games, books, sports equipment, clothing articles, comic books, or trading cards.
2. Each item then needs to be written on a piece of 3" x 5" paper with any information about it that is of importance. For example:

> Roller Blades
> size 8
> new wheels just installed

These papers or cards are the items with which they barter. The more cards they begin with, the more they have to barter with in class.

3. Allow the class to become a trading post for a certain amount of time each day for a specific number of days. Tell students that they are to barter and trade with others to try to better their lot of items. Encourage them to talk over possible trades and to work to convince others of the worth of an item.

4. After a specified amount of time, have students present to the class the items with which they began and ended. A quick vote will determine whether the class thought a student improved his/her lot or not. See who in the class is the real "horse trader."

5. Students will notice how hard it is to put value on an item when a standard of currency is not present. In fact, disagreements will develop over whether a student really did improve his/her lot or not. This can lead to a lesson on the purpose of currency in a world market.

Trades and Crafts

As an area settled and became more populated, demand for goods and services increased. This demand was met by pioneers who were not interested in making a living off the land but as tradesmen who could make a profit serving the population with a specialized craft. First among these would typically be a miller. Large mills were needed to grind grain in quantities greater than what the farmer did with his small hand mill. A gristmill could be set up several different ways. Owing to the abundance of rivers and streams east of the Mississippi, mills were often established next to a moving body of water. In some cases it was built on a barge and anchored in a river where the current could turn the wheel. In places lacking a reliable moving water source, mills were built that relied on the power of a team of horses walking on a treadmill.

Along with these grain mills, sawmills were established. Often the same machinery was used in the mill and parts were interchanged so that one mill could service both the lumbering and grinding needs of an area. Both these enterprises allowed for tremendous initial growth of an area. The gristmill was an integral part of the farmer's commerce and the sawmill provided lumber for plank houses. This attracted many more settlers who could now view the area as considerably more civilized if it was beyond the log cabin stage.

A number of other interesting trades developed in areas out of necessity. In the mid-nineteenth century, charcoal was in demand throughout New England for use in the refining of iron and steel. Men who specialized in making charcoal traveled throughout the countryside bartering for the wood found on farmer's lots. They would then chop it up, build large 30-foot-wide mounds of chopped woods covered with wet leaves and sod, and spend two weeks tending and controlling a very slow-burning fire in the mound, which would create charcoal. Sometimes known as *raggies*, these men were loners who were sometimes feared but respected by the local populace.

 FS-10140 Life as a Pioneer

Trades and Crafts continued

The influx of people into an area brought with it all those craftsmen who would service the household needs of the farmers as well. Cobblers set up shops or traveled around an area fitting shoes and repairing shoes of a family, often staying at one house for several days before moving on. In return for his services, he would receive room and board as well as goods he would need as he continued his travels. Often, cobblers doubled as harness makers and repairers.

Tinkers operated the same way. A tinker was a person who worked with shiny metals. He mended bowls, added new handles to cooking implements, and fashioned new cooking utensils from his bag of tools. With him he carried the molds to melt and cast pewter into plates, spoons, and bowls.

Coopers made barrels. They often spent time in apprenticeship before striking out on their own. They owned a large variety of tools for their craft and therefore usually required a more permanent setup. Barrels were the main means of storage for pioneers. In addition, they doubled for household furniture until more appropriate tables and chairs could be made. Barrels came in two types and many sizes. Some barrels had to be waterproof to hold rainwater, cider, or even stronger spirits. These were called *wet barrels. Dry barrels* held everything from flour to nails. A good cooper was always kept busy in a settled area.

In addition to the miller, the blacksmith was probably the next person to establish a business in a settled area. Named after the "black metal" he worked with, iron, the blacksmith provided all the tools and equipment needed on a farm, which was considerable. Simple hooks and nails, cutting tools, chains, wagon attachments, fireplace equipment, and huge kettles are a small sampling of the items which the blacksmith supplied the local farmers. It was hot, dirty, yet a much respected trade in any settlement. As with most trades, a blacksmith would perform all duties requested. That sometimes meant acting as a wheelwright, when called up to fix a broken wheel hub, or as a horseshoer (farrier) for the farmer's horse.

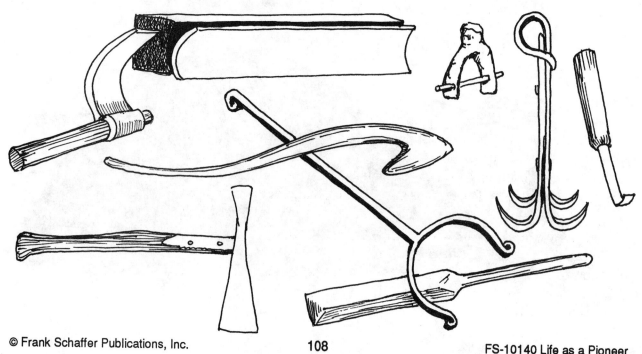

ACTIVITY — *Name That Tool*

The pioneer farmer had an abundance of farm tools which he used to plow, cultivate, plant, irrigate, harvest, and prepare his crop. Many of these tools would not be recognizable today because the average person has no use for them. This activity allows students to match the description of a tool with what it looked like. The answers are below.

1. jack hook
2. winnower
3. hay knife
4. barrel scorp
5. turn shoe hammer
6. ruggle

7. wagon jack
8. flail
9. cradle
10. wheelwright's reamer
11. swage
12. mill pick

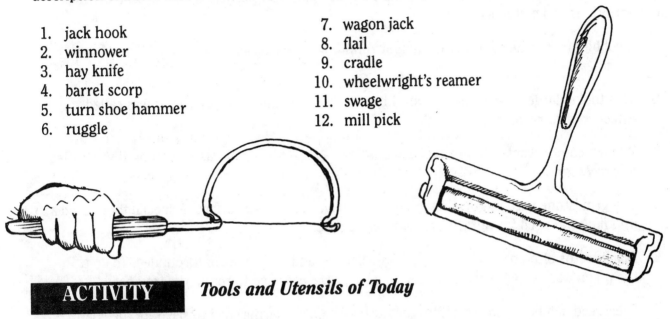

ACTIVITY — *Tools and Utensils of Today*

Although the tools of the pioneer might look somewhat strange to students today, it is only because they have never had to do a job that required such a tool. A pioneer would find many of today's tools equally as strange. In fact, many students probably could not recognize some simple utensils used today, such as an old-fashioned tea infuser or a C clamp.

Purpose:

To allow students to speculate on the uses of tools and utensils that appear odd or unusual.

Procedure:

1. Assign students the job of bringing in a tool or utensil from home that they think many students in class would not recognize. If a student's parent works in a trade that requires special tools, these are a great source.
2. Put these tools/utensils on a table or display them on desks and allow students to circulate and examine them. Encourage them not to divulge answers to keep others thinking. You can put labels on each tool to prevent confusion if they are moved during the examination.
3. Encourage students to make guesses when they do not know by carefully examining the parts and construction of the tool.
4. Allow the owner of the tool to identify it and explain its use and function.

NAME_____

Name That Tool

Directions:

Match the descriptions found on this page to the pictures of tools. There are no repeated sets and all descriptions and pictures are used.

A. A cobbler (shoemaker) used this tool for rounding shoe leather. It was called a *turn-shoe hammer*.

B. This tool enlarged the holes of a wheel hub so that it would fit on an axle. It was called a *wheelwright's reamer*.

C. When a cooper wanted to finish off the inside of a barrel he would use this tool. It was called a *barrel scorp*.

D. The grindstone used in grinding grain had to have a textured surface. A special tool called a *mill pick* was used to engrave this textured surface.

E. Blacksmiths often had to take a square-shaped bar and make part of it rounded. To do this the metal was heated. Then this tool called a *swage* was used to round the iron bar.

F. Once seed had been removed from the hull or chaff, the farmer had to separate the chaff. Picking it out was too time consuming, but since the hull was so much lighter than the seed he could toss it in the air and let the wind blow away the chaff as the heavier seed fell. A tool called a *winnower* was used to do this.

G. When a farmer took his grain to market in a wagon, he often had to cope with steep downhill slopes. To prevent the wagon from running over his horses, he attached this tool to the wheels. It was called a *ruggle*.

H. A farmer used this tool to not only cut the wheat but also to catch it as it fell so that it could be easily piled up. It was called a *cradle*.

I. Once hay was piled into huge haystacks it was hard to remove just a little without pulling the whole stack down. A tool called a *hay knife* was used to cut into the haystack and remove a portion of the hay.

J. To separate the wheat seed from the stalk it was pounded with this tool. It was called a flail.

K. To fix a broken axle the wheelwright had to jack up a wagon. This tool was called a *wagon jack*.

L. To remove large stones from his field by himself, a farmer used a *jack hook* and a long stick.

Directions:

Beside each picture of a tool used by a pioneer farmer or craftsman, write its name.

1	7
2	8
3	9
4	10
5	11
6	12

CHAPTER TEN

Family and Social Life

Social Evolution

The pioneers more or less rewrote the rule book when it came to family life. If we think that the colonists had broken the social traditions of European families, then we would certainly say that the pioneers completely buried what was left. Survival was the guiding principle for the first-wave pioneers. Social mores were of no use when grasshoppers as thick as clouds descended on a homestead. Traditional attitudes toward women that stood in the way when the field had to be plowed were easily forgotten. A boy became a man not according to some biological timeclock, but when the balance between being provided for tipped to being provider.

Only when civilization came to the West would it revert back to the more genteel ways of treating women and children. Despite efforts to "Easternize" the West, the mold that was broken in those harshest pioneer days never came back in quite the same fashion. Schools and education which were valued in the East were likewise valued in the West, but the style of education took on its own personality. Recreation, sport, and dancing, as well as courting and marriage, developed their own unique style in spite of every effort to soften the hard edges imposed by the pioneer environment.

Pioneer Women

Although popular history likes to assign the role of women as being secondary, it was hardly that. Men may have been in the vanguard of the westward movement, but women civilized it. Where men were content to live solitary, nomadic lives (note specifically the life style of trappers in the Rockies during the second and third quarter of the nineteenth century), women established roots that permitted a region to be settled. They did not just work alongside the trailblazing men but became the trailblazers themselves. The accounts of women establishing and holding homesteads are numerous. Between 1880 and 1910 over 12 percent of homesteaders in North Dakota were women. It is little coincidence, given the severe role that women played in the settling of the West, that the first state to allow women to vote was not found in the East, the South, nor the Midwest. It was in the very western state of Wyoming. In fact, when Wyoming was still a territory in 1869, women were given the vote, a full 50 years before the women's suffrage amendment was added to the Constitution.

To be certain, all pioneer women were not so hardy and individualistic. The prospect of walking the prairie to find dried buffalo dung for use in the stove was not for the weak of spirit. It demanded a woman with a true pioneer spirit. And it was this same spirit that refused to hide behind social custom or allow tradition to limit opportunity.

Getting students to look beyond stereotypes as they imagine the pioneer woman is no easy feat. Pioneer men are described in the context of their occupations and accomplishments, not within the context of a family. The inference is that they did the important work and domestic work was not the important work. Conversely, the pioneer woman is fully associated with doing "only" the domestic work. The pioneer woman, however, was commonly involved in all of the following:

1. breaking sod and plowing
2. handling all animals
3. harvesting
4. digging wells
5. repairing sod or log homes
6. making soap
7. slaughtering animals
8. keeping all financial records
9. smoking and preserving foods
10. hunting

It might be interesting to list these for students along with the traditional cooking, cleaning, and sewing and have students guess which were men's and which were women's duties. It provides an excellent introduction to the stereotype of the pioneer woman.

ACTIVITY   *A Survey of Attitudes Toward Women*

The attitude that Americans hold toward women is strikingly different than attitudes toward women in other cultures. Students can begin to explore the local attitudes toward women by devising their own survey.

Purpose:

To allow students to construct their own survey and gather data.

Procedure:

1. Target the subject.

    As a class, have students decide what kind of information they want to gather. A survey can be used to gather strictly factual data. For example, examine employment patterns among women in their own families.

    A survey can also be used to gather opinions and attitudes. For example, students may want to compare the contributions of female student council officers to those of male student council officers.

    A word of advice on targeting a subject: keep it simple. Too much data is impossible to interpret. Three to five basic bits of information are plenty for one survey.

2. Target the survey audience.

    Once students have decided on three to five core bits of information, they can target an audience to take the survey. The subject will undoubtedly determine the audience. Possible target audiences could be teachers, fellow students, parents, or even community members.

3. Construct the Survey Questions.

    For each question the class wants answered, design one or two survey questions. The questions can be one of three types:

    Yes - No questions—"Do you believe girls do as good a job on student councils as boys?"

    Quality questions—"Please rate the following jobs for their suitability for women."

    Open-ended questions—"What jobs have you held within the past five years?"

4. Administer the survey to the target audience. Each student can be equipped with X number of surveys and be responsible for gathering data.

5. Analyze the Results and Draw Conclusions

    Depending on the question type, students can tabulate yes and no responses, tally scores and averages, or read and interpret open-ended questions. Allow students to discuss these findings in small groups with each group drawing its own conclusions. The conclusions may prompt more investigation. Share the results with an interested group.

Pioneer Education

The history of the United States will attest that education has always been regarded with peculiar importance. During the sixteenth and seventeenth centuries colonies throughout the East made a point of establishing schools for their children. In the American frontier this tradition continued. As early as 1787, the Northwest Ordinance established that one section of each township was to be used to support public schools. By the time land was being offered inexpensively throughout Kansas, Nebraska, and Oklahoma, this attitude toward education still prevailed. In August of 1854 a group of emigrants reached Lawrence, Kansas, and five months later opened its first school. In 1871, with only four claims filed in Buffalo County, Nebraska, and people still living in railroad cars because their homes were not yet built, a group of homesteaders met after only eight days to discuss the organization of a school.

Certainly this would lead us to believe that the American pioneer was an educated person who held strong positive attitudes toward schooling. That image, however, flies in the face of the stereotyped illiterate pioneer who could barely read or write and held those that did with scorn and contempt. Survival of the fittest in the West did not seem to mean having a fit intellect.

Which image is true? They both are. The American settler valued education as a goal worthy of attainment to the point that he or she was willing to go to great lengths to make it available to others. In the world of the pioneer, however, schooling is not what fed the family or kept shelter over their heads. So we see unusual efforts to establish schools but much less effort to promote the education that was supposed to take place in them.

The Curriculum

In the Old Northwest only readin', 'ritin' and 'rithmetic were expected, and arithmetic was mostly just the four basic operations (known as ciphering). There were, of course, no standardized texts. Students were asked to bring whatever book might be at home. A collection of Bibles, *Pilgrim's Progress*, and almanacs would usually arrive. From this, the teacher had to instruct everyone. Slates were basically unknown.

There were no requirements for attendance beyond what a family might require. Children who were especially obstinate about attending probably got out of school earlier than others. No laws forced them to attend. School was run during winter months only allowing the children to be home when planting and harvesting were required.

Sixty years later in the plains frontier the curriculum had made changes. Geography, astronomy, grammar, spelling, and penmanship were added to the curriculum depending on the settlement and teacher. In some locations students were still bringing the books, but by 1836 William H. McGuffey had established his McGuffey Reading Series that most everyone was using. It contained poems laced with moral lessons.

By the last half of the nineteenth century, students were more expected to attend schools. They at least needed to show some proficiency in reading and writing and arithmetic before being allowed to leave. Often they grew out of school as soon as they could hold a job or do the work of an adult. School was held only about five months out of the year, still keeping children free to help with planting and harvesting. No laws outside of local ones mandated school.

The Teacher

The schoolmaster of the Old Northwest in the early nineteenth century was usually male. He was also less respected in the community than his apparent position would warrant. Often he was a drifter who agreed to be the school master to tide him over for the winter. He might have been a drunk. He was often homeless. Few checked his credentials for teaching beyond whether he could read and write himself. The phrase "Those who cannot do . . . teach." applied well to this person. He would typically teach for a fee assessed per child ($1.00 per child was common). He often stayed in the homes of the pupils he taught as part of the arrangement for teaching them. If he lasted one winter and stayed for the next, it was unusual. A student's education was often interrupted for lack of a teacher and resumed only when another was found.

By the last half of the nineteenth century, this situation had improved, but not by much. More schoolteachers of the plains were now women, who used the wages earned to supplement their living. They were consequently less inclined to be of the derelict variety and more inclined to stay in an area for several years as schoolteacher. Their own education, however, was often little more than that of the students they taught. Certification standards might have been no more than a quick verbal quiz by the state superintendent, who would travel around from county to county to inspect and recertify teachers. Payment had not increased much, and thus the position of the schoolteacher in the community was one of cordial, not earnest, respect.

ACTIVITY   *School Then and Now*

Few students realize that the education standards of today are so much more stringent than at any time in our country's history. An easy exercise for students to perform is to have them interview other teachers in the school to find out what is required to become a teacher, and then examine school documents such as curriculum guides to establish those standards. The findings can then be made into a chart which can be displayed in contrast to the information below.

Category	Old Northwest	Plains Frontier
Gender of Teacher	typically male	evenly split
Certification Requirements	ability to read and write only	quizzed by state superintendent
Salary	$1.00/student plus room and board	@ $20.00/month room and board
Discipline	whipping expected	whipping allowed
Curriculum	Reading, writing, math operations	reading, writing, math operations
Books and Equipment	none or whatever students brought	McGuffey's Reader
Length of Day	unknown	8 to 10 hours
Length of Year	winter months only	average of five months per year
Attendance Requirements	no requirement	no requirements beyond what a family or community set

Work and Play

The first wave of pioneers were as isolated from civilization as any could be. For some, that was the life that they chose and preferred. In fact, as more settlers entered an area, many first-wave pioneers would pick up and leave to avoid the "crowding" of having neighbors so close a person might hear their rifles while out hunting.

The second wave of pioneers to an area were usually more sociable. By today's standards, they, too, lived in isolation. It was not an isolation they relished, so it was a condition that they sought to remedy as often as possible. This was true in the settling of the Old West (east of the Mississippi River) as well as the New West (west of the Mississippi). The distances people lived from one another were certainly barriers to socializing on any kind of regular basis, but often these settlers were more than willing to travel the better part of a day to get together with others. The real obstacle to socialization was the daily work load of the settler.

Carving out a living in the frontier was a sunup to sundown proposition, and even after sundown, time could be spent in front of the fireplace using its light to make gunshot or mend clothing. Given such a life style, it is understandable that most early recreation activities centered around work.

When a new barn had to be raised or a new cabin needed building for a family who had recently arrived, word went throughout an area and soon neighbors would arrive to help with the "log raisin'." No one would refuse to give help since everyone's existence depended on help from neighbors from time to time. These events were more than just more work. They were occasions for socializing. The hosts provided the whiskey and whatever food they could afford. The guests provided food as well and the manpower to get the job done.

Community work became an institution very quickly in an area. From log raising it was not far to corn husking bees. When a crop came in, the entire settlement might meet at someone's home to husk the corn. In some instances a game was made of it with the pile being divided into two equal shares and the huskers being likewise divided into two teams. At the word "go" the teams would husk away with the goal to husk their pile first. There was laughter, conversation, food and drink, and the need to socialize was being fulfilled. As civilization crept into a settlement, these husking bees would become more sedate. Both men and women would participate. The competition would relax, and new traditions evolved. One such tradition involved having the man or woman who husked a red ear of corn being afforded the opportunity to kiss the person of his or her choice. Many a man came to such a bee with a red ear already available and hidden.

The Bee

A bee was any social gathering that combined work with competition and/or amusement. Finding work in a pioneer setting was never hard and since, as the old saying goes, "Two hands are better than one," bees of all sorts developed. There were husking bees, quilting bees, threshing and harvesting bees, and fulling parties. *Fulling* consisted of saturating new cloth in hot soapsuds and laying it out on the puncheon floor of the cabin. Then, women sitting in a circle stomped on the fabric with bare feet. This process was said to eliminate shrinkage after the cloth was made into clothing. Later, bees were even incorporated into frontier schooling, with the spelling bee becoming a popular competitive activity in the 1870s and 1880s. At the end of a school year, one school would send out invitations to other schools to be a part of a spelldown. Not only did the students take part but the entire community would arrive to cheer their team on.

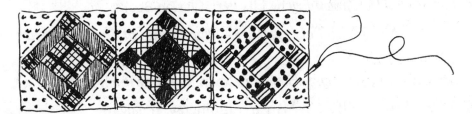

To Bee or Not to Bee

Students today have so many varied opportunities to socialize that a bee is unnecessary. The pioneers relied one another to accomplish tasks that may have otherwise been impossible or overwhelming alone. Today's system of services-for-hire nearly eliminates the need for this type of cooperation. Only in geographically secluded parts of the United States do we still see this type of activity in some form.

Purpose:

Students will recognize aspects of their lives that would have required bees during pioneer days and speculate on daily activities that could be incorporated into a bee today.

Procedure:

1. Using the Yellow Pages, have students go through it and list services that are available because the job is one that requires the collaboration between several people. These would include large jobs such as cement laying or tree removal as opposed to simple lawn care or housekeeping.

2. Share those lists in class. See if anyone in class has ever had those jobs done by neighbors or friends instead of hiring someone to do it. Discuss how the job became a social event as well.

3. Since bees were sometimes competitive, have students list aspects of their studies which could be made into a bee. Have students design and host one of these bees. Examples could include: math bees, spelling bees, or historical dates bee.

LITERATURE FOR STUDENTS

Reading can be integrated with any unit on the pioneers. The books listed below include literature that is both fiction and nonfiction. The average reading levels are appropriate for middle school students. They are listed alphabetically by title.

Nonfiction

1. *Frontier Dreams:* Life on the Great Plains by Catherine E. Chambers. Troll Associates.

2. *Frontier Living* by Edwin Tunis. HarperCollins Children's Books.

3. *Hunter's Stew, and Hangtown Fry* by Lila Perl. Clarion Books.

4. *Husking Quiltings and Barn Raising: Work—Play Parties in Early America* by Victoria Sherrow. Walker & Co.

5. *Nineteenth Century Clothing* by Bobbie Kalman. Crabtree Publications.

6. *Settlers in the American West* by Margaret Killingray. Trafalgar.

7. *Wagons West: Trail Tales* by Robert Shellenberger. Heritage West.

Biography

1. *Gallery of Pioneers* by Ann K. Cooper. Edit Heliodor.

2. *Great Figures of the Wild West* by Paul Walker. Facts on File.

3. *Jane Long: Frontier Woman* by Ann F. Crawford. Benson Publications.

4. *Kentucky Frontiersman: The Adventures of Henry Ware, Hunter and Border Fighter* by Joseph A. Altsheler. Voyager Publications.

Fiction

1. *The Bone Wars* by Katheryn Laskey. Puffin Books.

2. *Carlotta* by Scott O'Dell. Viking Child Books.

3. *Leaving Eldorado* by Joann Mazzio. Houghton Mifflin.

4. *Pioneers Go West* by George R. Stewart. Random Books.

5. *Sign of the Beaver* by Elizabeth George Speare. Dell Pub.

6. *West Against the Wind* by Liza K. Murrow. Holiday.

COMPUTER PROGRAMS RELATED
TO PIONEER HISTORY

Below is a listing of computer software that can be integrated with the study of pioneer life. Some of the software deals with the pioneer time period exclusively, while other deals with skills students use in learning to investigate this era. Included with each entry is is the title, publishing company, computer format, and a brief synopsis. Computer format abbreviations are:

Apple II—software that runs on Apple II with a 5.25" drive
Apple II GS—software that runs on Apple II GS with a 3.5" drive
PC—software that runs on MS/DOS with 5.25" drive
PC 3.5—software that runs on MS/DOS with a 3.5" drive
MAC—software that runs on a Macintosh Computer

1. *The Forty-Niners*. ENTREX. Apple II, Apple II GS, PC, PC 3.5. This simulation program has students traveling across America to the gold fields, seeking gold, and staking a claim.

2. *The Indian Wars*. ENTREX. Apple II, Apple II GS, PC, PC 3.5. Students choose a side in this historical struggle between settlers and the U.S. cavalry and the Indians who hold the land.

3. *The Texas Revolution*. ENTREX. Apple II, Apple II GS, PC, PC 3.5. Students relive the revolution of the Texans against the army of Santa Anna in this simulation.

4. *The War on the Indians*. Focus Media. Apple II, PC. Similar to *The Indian Wars,* this simulation has students investigating the circumstances and controversy between the U.S. and the native Americans during the move westward.

5. *Wagons West*. Focus Media. Apple II. A simulation that leads students to understand the motivations of settlers for moving west as well as the obstacles they faced in traveling and settling.

6. *Oregon Trail*. MECC. Apple II, Apple II GS, PC, MAC. Students simulate being a settler on the Oregon Trail and must buy supplies, decide on routes, hunt for food, and perform many other duties in an effort to make it to Oregon. Student decisions can lead to success or failure.

7. *Race for the West*. ENTREX. Apple II, Apple II GS, PC, PC 3.5 In this simulation students compete against other countries such as France in an effort to explore the northwestern United States.

8. *The American Journal Series: The Alamo and Lewis and Clark*. K-12 Micromedia Publishing. MAC. Both these data bases provide students with accounts surrounding the two events. Interactive maps, and calendars are provided.

AN INDEX OF ACTIVITIES

The index found on the following pages is a guide to student activities developed for each chapter. This index is designed to act as a quick reference for finding a specific activity. It is also intended to be a planning guide by providing a list of subjects and skills that each activity involves. Most of the categories are self-explanatory. Additional notes are included below.

Art relates to all activities that allow students to design, draw, diagram, or develop something visual. Bulletin board and craft activities are all labeled with the AR symbol.

Critical Thinking involves skills such as evaluating, productive thinking, planning, and decision making.

Cooking as well as some art activities have a math label since measuring is a part of the process.

Researching relates to any activity that has students participating in traditional research such as using reference material as well as nontraditional research such as interviewing or observing.

Speaking/listening is identified for all activities that have students presenting information to the class, discussing information in a group, or contacting outside sources in an interview.

As you use the activities, you may find yourself changing them to fit your specific plans. As you do, you will find that new skills and subjects will be incorporated into each activity. Below is the key to all abbreviations used in this index

AR = Art
CO = Cooking
CT = Critical Thinking
SL = Speaking/Listening

HE = Health
MA = Math
RE = Research
* = denotes activities that include reproducible student pages

SC = Science
SS = Social Studies
WR= Writing

CHAPTER-BY-CHAPTER ACTIVITY INDEX

Chapter Six—Hunting for Food

Chapter Seven—What the Pioneers Ate and How They Prepared Their Food

Chapter Eight - Health and Medicine

Chapter Nine—Making a Living

Chapter Ten—Family and Social Life